WORKING IT OUT

WORKING IT OUT

The Domestic Double Standard

Judith K. Sprankle

Walker and Company
New York

First published in the United States of America in 1986 by the Walker Publishing Company, Inc.

Published simultaneously in Canada by John Wiley & Sons Canada, Limited, Rexdale, Ontario.

Library of Congress Cataloging-in-Publication Data

Sprankle, Judith K., 1946–
Working it out.

1. Women—United States—Social conditions.
2. Work and family—United States. 3. Wives—Employment—United States. 4. Women—United States—Time management. I. title.
HQ1426.S666 1986 305.4 85-26460
ISBN 0-8027-0883-8

Printed in the United States of America

10 9 8 7 6 5 4 3 2 1

To Rosemary, an exceptional lady,
whose friendship and integrity have done more
to renew my faith in human nature than I can ever tell her.

TABLE OF CONTENTS

PREFACE

Women like me, who came of age during the late 1960s and early 1970s, were encouraged in that first stage of the women's movement to "have it all"—to combine marital, maternal, and career responsibilites into one manageable, even enjoyable, lifestyle. But what, ten or more years later, is the reality?

For the vast majority of today's working women, from Jane Pauley to Jane Doe, "having it all" might more accurately be characterized as "having to do it all." Despite the good intentions of a husband or significant other, it is rare that domestic responsibilites are in fact shared equally. While he pitches in on the home front sporadically, his first priority, by and large, continues to be his job. She, on the other hand, is expected to do domestic duty whether it's convenient or not, often to the detriment of her career, to which her employer expects her to give the same time, energy, and commitment as her unfettered male counterparts.

Shared responsibility within the home is the ideal, but it is rarely the reality. The school or day-care center calls Mom when Johnny is running a fever, not Dad. If the house is filmed with dust and the laundry bin is overflowing, it is she who is perceived to be slovenly, not he. If he fixes breakfast for the family on Sunday morning, he's a hero, but if the eggs aren't scrambled punctually Monday through Saturday, she's a slacker. He's a model father if he takes Junior to the once-a-month Cub Scout pack meeting, but she's falling down on the job if the boy doesn't appear at weekly den meetings on time, with the right change for dues, in a clean uniform, and with every blessed badge and arrow sewn—by her—in place.

Plainly put, the woman of the house is never off the hook. While we have made progress in terms of employment opportunities, the double standard clearly lives on in the domestic areas of our lives. So how is today's woman working it out?

Within these pages, the reality of having (to do) it all is explored via the experiences of dozens of working wives and mothers who represent a wide variety of ages, income brackets, educational backgrounds, and job categories. While committed to abolishing the domestic double standard in future generations, they have learned to live with it, for the present, by devising practical strategies to temper its effects.

Working It Out illustrates by example the possibilities for coping with a complicated, but rewarding, lifestyle as these loving and intelligent women reveal how they are managing to enjoy their hectic lives against all odds. Instead of being preached at by experts, you will be welcomed into a circle of your peers who have "been there"—indeed, who still *are* there—and who have found positive ways to deal with multiple roles. It is my hope that you will feel as though you have encountered dozens of new friends with whom you can identify and from whom you can gain both practical help and moral support as we all confront the issues of the domestic double standard, in this second stage of the women's movement, with strength, humor, and a lot of love.

JUDITH K. SPRANKLE
Newington, Connecticut

1

DEFINITIONS

Like a weed which threatens to choke all that is bright and good in the lives of contemporary women, the domestic double standard flourishes despite our decades-long struggle for equality.

Before we can yank it firmly from amid the opportunities now flowering around us, we must acquaint ourselves with the impressive root system that has allowed the DDS to thrive throughout the first stage of the women's movement.

What we had hoped would evolve into the New Marriage crumbled in the face of the New Reality. Publicly, we prided ourselves on our Superwoman image, while privately, we mourned the death of our great expectations.

GREAT EXPECTATIONS

AT THE DAWN OF CREATION, Eve may have set one of womankind's most unfortunate precedents when she offered Adam that apple. With one ill-considered action, she set the pace for every succeeding generation, in which woman cooks and man asks, "What's for dinner, Honey?"

One cannot help but wonder how it all might have turned out had Adam chosen the menu that day, but second guessing is an unproductive occupation, at best. The fact is, the concept of "woman's work" has endured thousands of years of societal and political upheaval, in this country and the majority of others, largely intact. While women have gained the right to vote, have been accepted reluctantly into traditionally male occupations, and are slowly but steadily carving places for themselves in the upper echelons of business and government, the old double standard lives on in the domestic arena and will for some years to come. The woman who wears a hard hat on the construction site each day still dons an apron each night.

It's a complex issue, but for those of us in the post-World War II generation, its roots lie somewhere in our turbulent coming of age. Graduating from high school in the mid-to-late 1960s, we were immediately confronted by our militant older sisters who insisted that we abandon the mores and models instilled in us by our well-meaning parents. No longer should we expect our men to open the car door—or any door, for that matter—or to leap to their feet when we entered a room. Far from being forbidden, premarital sex became a rite of passage. Gone, too, was the 1950s model of domestic bliss: marriage to a college-educated husband, two children and two cars, and a lifetime of volunteer work.

"Good riddance!" we exulted, once we recovered from our initial shock, and promptly set about creating a brand new, equally unsatisfactory model for ourselves: the uncommitted, open-ended relationship.

Living together *sans* benefit of clergy, open marriages in which partners were free to engage in casual couplings with others, and other modern relationships became the rule rather than the exception. They created the illusion of unfettered love between two independent, consenting adults, and they lasted just about as long as they deserved to. While struggling to maintain an equal footing with our male counterparts and to abolish the double standard in the work place as well as in the bedroom, we accepted, however briefly, the new "no strings" arrangements. We buried our nagging doubts about the value of casual sexual liaisons to our lives, suppressed our rage when our partners took us at our word about being free to come and go, and refused to admit our longing for committed men with whom to share our lives—with whom to build satisfying lives together.

That model died hard, but die it did, as men and women acknowledged their need for roots—a home base from which to venture forth each morning and take our chances in the world and a loving partner who would welcome us back each evening and help us assess the day's damages. For many of us, this meant family, the old fashioned, "'til death do us part" commitment we had so recently scorned. Bravely, women resolved to stop wasting their time on casual relationships and made their newly acknowledged wishes known to a surprising number of similarly inclined men.

Still, we were reluctant to abandon the positive aspects of our decade of freedom. We had enjoyed, to a certain extent, our independence, reveling in our newfound strengths and abilities. We had found satisfaction in earning our own livings and had discovered a new world of challenging, stimulating career opportunities open to us. We wanted commitment from our men, but we also wanted it clear that some choices were still ours to make: when and if we would bear children, where and how long we would work outside the home, and with whom we would continue to socialize. Naturally, we would consider the wishes of our partners, but no longer would we bow to their preferences.

Secure in our new identities, we sallied forth to negotiate the terms of yet a third preposterous model: the fifty-fifty marriage.

For me, as for so many other women, the years 1965–1969 were a time of trial. Scorning a bachelor's degree as a frivolous credential, and desperate to establish myself as an independent entity, I waved aside my parents' offer of a college education and opted instead for a year of secretarial training at Katharine Gibbs School in Boston.

Because it is New England's preeminent college town, housing hundreds of thousands of undergraduates from all over the world in the dormitories and apartments of Boston University, Northeastern, Tufts, Harvard, Boston College, Radcliffe, MIT, and dozens of other institutions from September to June each year, Boston is a melting pot of youthful society. Still, it is old New England, which may explain why the flower children of that era preferred Berkeley to Back Bay and why, though we embraced portions of the Hippie culture, we did so more cautiously. Beer, not pot, was the mainstay of the Boston fraternity party in the mid-sixties; and while we were sexually active, we abided by an unwritten code of discretion.

Flo, Gina, Joanne, Pepper, Nancy, Marta. Their very names—as well as those of their countless beaux, for all of us were endlessly in love—evoke memories of another self, the not-yet-me self who struggled to put aside the values of the past and to find a new, more satisfactory model for the future. To my recollection, and certainly to our credit, not one of us aspired to find a man and acquire an engagement ring. We were there, toiling over our typewriters and steno pads, to equip ourselves to earn a living, and by and large, we did. We would be whatever we chose to be, unshackled by husbands and babies; and though we enjoyed our lovers thoroughly that year, we were always secretly relieved when they moved on.

In June, we too moved on, scattering to New York, Washington, D.C., San Francisco, and Denver to explore our options in the work place. October of 1966 found me in San Jose, California, at a then innovative university-based educational television station, where I became, to my everlasting disgust, the 19-year-old mascot of the department. My boss—an earthy, energetic fifty-year-old woman named Gaither Lee "Terry" Martin from Lubbock, Texas—hired me primarily, she later confided, "to give the boys something to look at," but defended my by then questionable virtue like a bulldog. Whenever I drooped in after a falling-out with my latest swain, she would help me regain my perspective and my sense of humor with one of her Texas homilies. "Now, I like men better'n I like chocolate candy, Honey," she would say, "but I could always take 'em or leave 'em both."

In her own inimitable way, that lady taught me more about standing up for myself in a man's world than she ever knew. Striding confidently through her days, she never let me see the difficulties and discrimination she must have endured at that time. Just being the department head in an emerging field would have been rigorous enough, but as the female boss of an all-male crew in the late sixties, she faced an extraordinary challenge. And with a shrug and a joke, she made it all look easy, dismissing the double standard in the workplace as mere nonsense.

The lives of most women of Terry's generation, however, revolved around their husbands' careers. During the early days of World War II, for example, my mother married the business manager of a hospital where she worked as a nurse. A year later, however, Dad chucked the administrative life to open his own service station, and their lives were defined largely by his extraordinary work schedule for the next thirty-three years. He worked six and a half days a week, often until the station closed at 9:00 P.M., because he loved it. On Sunday afternoons, he might mow the lawn, and he'd help with the dinner dishes if he were home during the week, but that was about it for him in terms of domestic work. Mom did everything else, from weekly cleaning and yard work to major painting and repairs, aided only by me and my sister, even after she returned to nursing. We got an exceptionally good grounding in home maintenance as a result, but it was hardly fun for any of us. It would have been nice, I think, to have had Dad around more. But it was also nice, for Mom and for us, to have the man of the family so happy in his chosen work. So it was, as such things usually are, a compromise.

With that as my background, I was aware, though subliminally, that whatever else a woman might do, she still bore the lion's share of the responsibility for homemaking. And however many love affairs I and my contemporaries had, it was we who cooked the cosy little suppers and washed the shirts and sewed on the buttons—and somewhere, deep in our souls, resented it.

On the career front, things were not going so swimmingly either. Though we relished our ability to support ourselves, we began to notice that the men with whom we had graduated only a few years before were nimbly climbing the corporate ladders, while we remained behind our typewriters and waited for someone to notice that we had a great deal more to offer. And finally, we got tired of waiting.

The women's movement combined with the Vietnam War in a blur of activism over the next few years. Feeling out of control as a society, we turned to each other as individuals to reassert some control over our personal destinies, abandoning the uncommitted relationships of the sixties as we struggled to impose some order on our lives and our futures. Marriage was no longer a dirty word, but negotiation often replaced the romantic scenario in which he popped the question, and she responded with a breathless, "Yes!" In the early seventies, she was as likely to pop the question as he, and the response from either party was likely to be, "Yes . . . if we can work it out."

Reluctant to take a step backwards into the role of chief cook and bottle washer, or to be viewed by our partners as sex objects and breeders, women set out to create a modern version of matrimony: the fifty-fifty marriage. I know. I was one of them; and for a while, it really seemed possible. So long as things were clearly understood from the start, we believed, we could keep the ground we had gained on the work front and start making inroads on the household front, as well. Shared responsibility in every area—financial, domestic, and parental—was the goal, and eagerly, we set out to attain it with the cooperation of our newly enlightened male partners.

In early 1970, I met a man with whom I wanted to share my life. Following a succession of spoiled, selfish lotharios, Wayne embodied everything I sought in a partner. Bright, warm, funny, open-minded, and tolerant, he seemed able to accept my wishes for a career as well as a home and family—even to support them. After living together for several months, we decided to marry, work for several years while sharing domestic responsibilities, then think about starting a family.

Wayne was a pharmacist, a profession that offered security plus mobility, and I was an executive secretary. We earned exactly the same salary that first year, $10,000 each. While the world was in turmoil around us, we set up housekeeping in an apartment on the outskirts of Hartford, Connecticut, banked lots of money, took trips to Bermuda and Puerto Rico and the Bahamas, and smugly congratulated ourselves on having it all figured out. Our lives, we were certain, would be exceptional—no middle-class mediocrity for us, no sir. On our first anniversary, we rented a posh suite at the local Hilton and renewed our fifty-fifty marriage contract over a bottle of champagne. It was working, and we'd make damn sure it went right on working.

For the next few years, all went relatively smoothly. In 1971, we bought a modest house in the suburbs and continued our modern lifestyle, meticulously sharing everything from the vacuuming to the snow shoveling in the interests of fair play. But in the spring of that year, Wayne became disenchanted with the role of the modern pharmacist, which consisted mainly of counting pills and typing labels, and decided to pursue a career in drug enforcement, with my wholehearted support. Blithely, I sent him off to the Drug Enforcement Administration's training school in Washington, D.C., and cheerfully, I accepted DEA's mandate that agents be willing to relocate whenever such moves were in the Administration's best interests. And if significant overtime was involved with the job, well, I could handle it. It would be worth it, after all, to have a husband who was happy in his work.

With Wayne enthusiastically pursuing his new profession, however, it was impossible to ignore my own frustration on the job. I had been a secretary for too long, and without that bachelor's degree I had declined to get back in 1965, other opportunities remained closed to me. Not that I didn't try to climb out of the clerical trenches, mind you. I did, but without success. The futility of my effort was never clearer to me than it was on the day I entered the personnel department of a major Hartford corporation and noted two entrances to the inner office. One was marked, "Four-year Degree Holders Only," and the second, "Others." Shocked and humiliated, I slunk from the building to consider a future in which I would be an "Other," and found it unacceptable. "Screw them," I thought, and went home to find a way to beat the system.

There was a way, as it turned out—a new approach to post-secondary education called the External Degree. Instead of enduring four solid years of college classes, I could earn college credits through independent study. If I could pass the same examinations required of all graduates of the State University of New York, I would be granted the same degree: a Bachelor of Science in Business Administration. I promptly enrolled, but I was not content to remain a secretary while I earned my degree. Instead, I decided to open my own book store and become a stunningly successful entrepreneur.

With Wayne's uncritical support, I spent 1974–75 losing $22,000 of our hard-earned money on what turned out to be a disastrous retail operation. Within months of the store's opening, a mammoth mall opened five miles from the little shopping center in which I operated. Two major bookstore chains occupied prominent positions in the mall and made quick work of driving every independent bookstore owner in the metropolitan area, including me, out of business. Narrowly escaping bankruptcy, I retreated from the business world once more, broke, depressed, and about two months pregnant.

Though my pregnancy took us by surprise, since two locally noted urologists had assured us that Wayne was all but sterile, we were delighted. Just about everything else had gone wrong in my life, but biological lightning had struck, granting us the opportunity we thought had been denied us to become parents. With that wonderful prospect, I philosophically returned to secretarial work, accepting temporary assignments to help pay off the residual book store debts, and awaited the birth of our son in November 1975. We attended Lamaze classes together, and Wayne was ecstatically present to welcome Ricky when he arrived, right on schedule.

While the prenatal instruction had prepared me for the

birth, I was shockingly ill informed about the reality of having a new baby in my life. Rarely having babysat as a teenager, I scarcely knew which end of an infant to diaper, let alone how to deal with a severely colicky newborn who screamed day and night for more than four months. It's a period in my life I still cannot recall without flinching, a blur of chronic fatigue. In those pre-paternity-leave days, Wayne was able to take only a week's vacation time to share the burden of those endless nights. After that, it was up to me, and I became the neighborhood zombie.

Though the worst of the colic subsided by the time Ricky was five months of age, his erratic sleep pattern seemed unalterable, and I continued to wake four, five, who knows how many times a night to his unhappy wailing. Desperate for some relief, and still guilt-ridden about our burden of debt from my failed business, I accepted a full-time secretarial job when Ricky was seven months old and hired a wonderful, grandmotherly neighbor to care for him during the day. My second week on the job, I discovered I was pregnant again, and I spent the evening sobbing through *That's Entertainment* at the local movie house, wishing I had died instead of the rabbit.

By the time Jenna joined us in May of 1977, however, I had arrived at some sort of acceptance of my new situation. Wayne and I had longed for children, and now, by heaven, we had them. Enough, however, was enough, and Wayne—having been told two years earlier that there was no way he would ever sire a child—had a vasectomy. Although Ricky continued his wakeful habits, Jenna was the perfect baby, snoring her way placidly through the nights. Our debt had been reduced to the point where we could manage the monthly payments on Wayne's paycheck, though just barely. We still had the house, our health, and each other, and surely, Ricky would sleep through the night at some point before he entered college. It was simply a matter of hanging in, so I settled in for the duration.

While I mixed formula, folded diapers, and doggedly continued to complete the requirements for my bachelor's degree, however, I clung stubbornly to the belief that this domestic interlude was merely that—a hiatus in the normal course of things caused by an unfortunate business experience and a biological fluke. Because Wayne was now earning twice what I could as a secretary, his primary role had to to be that of breadwinner; and because of our remaining debt, for which I felt responsible, we could not afford to hire help. So the domestic responsiblity would, for the moment, have to be mine. When I earned my degree and paid off the last of the book store debt, our fifty-fifty marriage would bloom anew, I felt sure. So I finished my studies, wrote the final check to the bank, and made a fresh start in the fall of 1977, accepting my first "professional" position: Director of Public Relations for the Metropolitan Hartford YWCA.

In retrospect, I see that year as the turning point in our relationship. Having finally dragged myself out of the secretarial trenches, I felt in command of my professional destiny for the first time. No longer an "other" in the eyes of corporate personnel directors, I would now catch up with my male counterparts. The children were thriving during the work week under the loving supervision of a young mother with two children of her own who preferred staying at home to an outside job. Weekends were a marathon of housecleaning, grocery shopping, pediatric appointments, and visits to Grandma, but we were surviving.

What I failed to see—or perhaps, to admit—during that hectic year was how drastically Wayne's and my roles had altered on the domestic front. The demands of his career as a federal law-enforcement officer, which we had so cheerfully accepted Before Children, now intruded harshly into our lives. He was required to work sixty hours a week, for openers, and additional overtime was frequently required by specific investigations. I never knew from one day to the next when or if he would be home. He was on call more weekends than he was free, and a social life was next to impossible because of his constantly changing schedule. Two or three times a year, he traveled to Canada, the Mexican border, the Florida coast, or wherever the international drug trade demanded; and two-week stints at special training schools in Georgia became customary. So while Wayne pitched in at home when he was there, I could never plan on his availability and was therefore 100 percent responsible for the running of the household, whether or not I actually ended up performing every task.

It was nobody's fault, but I was never off the hook—a fact, I realized only after juggling my full-time job and the brunt of the domestic burden for more than a year, with which I would have to live for a long, long time. As the 1970s drew to a close, I publicly prided myself on my Superwoman image and privately mourned the death of our great expectations.

While the specifics of those interesting years varied from marriage to marriage, I now know that the bottom line for most young couples in the late 1970s was essentially the same. Though their efforts to arrive at an equitable division of domestic and income-producing responsibilities were sincere, circumstances eventually undermined them, leaving him caught in the sticky web of his employer's demands and her holding the domestic bag, right along with her full-time job, which had, more often than not, become an economic necessity.

The circumstances in which the 1970s woman struggled for domestic and employment equality very often approximated those of her 1950s sister, and she found herself having to put personal needs and priorties second to those of her husband. In the '50s, a woman married to an aspiring lawyer, dentist, or physician—professions requiring extended and expensive schooling followed by years of financial struggle—frequently took a job to meet expenses until her husband's practice was successfully launched. But the '50s woman knew it would be a short-term sacrifice—an investment of time and energy that would ultimately pay off not only in financial security but in personal freedom. In contrast, the 1970s wife in the same situation soon found that the economic repercussions of inflation made it impossible to predict when, or even if, she would be able to pursue her own goals, once having shelved them in favor of her husband's.

Take Melanie and Dennis, for instance, who met in their junior year at the University of Connecticut, where she majored in business administration and he in pre-med. Though both, as it happened, were from outside the state, they opted to settle in Connecticut when they married in 1974. "We had our bachelor's degrees by then," Melanie recalls, "but Dennis still had four years of dental school to go, even if he didn't specialize. Our parents had extended themselves about as far as they could financially to get us that far, so the rest of the trip was on us."

More specifically, it turned out to be on Melanie, who went to work immediately following graduation to support herself and Dennis while he tackled the next demanding four-year stint in his medical education. She says, "In Connecticut, probably one out of every six workers is employed by an insurance company, many of which are headquartered in the Hartford region, and I soon became one of them. I started out in the Personnel Department of a huge insurer, working my way up from receptionist to secretary, to test administrator. By the time Dennis finished his education, I was an apprentice interviewer. I really enjoyed working with people face-to-face on a daily basis and helping them evaluate their job skills and career goals. At the same time, though, I couldn't wait for Dennis to finish school. His tuition expenses kept us pretty well strapped, so we lived in a seedy third-floor walk-up in East Hartford and drove an old Buick that probably should have been retired as junk even before we bought it. I was tired of working hard, making good career progress, and still living like paupers. I wanted Dennis to take his turn at supporting us so I could have a baby."

To the couple's dismay, however, their financial woes were only beginning once Dennis finally passed his exams. The cost of setting up and equipping a dental practice was extraordinary, and they were immediately confronted with $100,000 in debt, offset only by the unknown amount of income Dennis's first patients would generate. "The early years of any practice are an iffy proposition," Dennis points out. "The start-up costs are overwhelming, and the amount of income is unpredictable. Some practices take right off, but others have to be built slowly over a period of years. You just can't tell. Melanie and I had really scrimped so that we would end up even when I finished dental school—no savings, but no big debts, either. It seemed so unfair that there was no reward, just another huge loan to pay off. I really wanted her to have a chance to stay at home and have a baby, but there was just no way."

"We had both always wanted a large family," Melanie continues, "with at least four children. That was one reason why Dennis chose dentistry. It seemed to be a lucrative enough profession to support even a large family. Boy, were we dumb! Anyway, by this time, I was twenty-six years old, really ready to have a baby, and extremely frustrated to discover that I would have to postpone that dream for years longer."

It was partly that frustration, in fact, that led to a further complication in the couple's financial picture. Her major desire thwarted, Melanie convinced Dennis to snatch at a chance to fulfill their next major goal, buying a home of their own, when they learned of a gracious suburban house about to come on the market at an exceptionally good price. "The seller had recently been widowed, and he couldn't bear to stay in the house where he and his wife had spent so many happy years. He didn't seem to care much what he got for it as long as he could sell it quickly, but he did care who bought the house. He wanted it to go to some nice young couple, he said, who wanted a real home and lots of kids—and there we were!" Melanie recalls. "The problem was, of course, that unless he wanted to give us the house, we couldn't afford it."

Knowing of their daughter's long-standing wish for a

house, however, Melanie's parents made an unexpected, but characteristically generous, offer. "Mom and Dad had just sold their big colonial in Massachusetts, preferring to retire to a luxury condominium that required less upkeep. They had made quite a handsome profit on the house sale, so they told us, "Why should you wait to inherit the money when you can really use it now?" and gave us the down payment for the house we wanted! It seemed like a miracle . . . until we moved in and realized the true expense involved in maintaining a house."

Still burdened with debt from setting up Dennis's practice, the couple quickly became acquainted with outrageous heating bills, insurance premiums, and the cost of replacing ancient appliances when they failed, plus monthly mortgage and tax payments. At age twenty-seven, Melanie began to despair of ever being able to quit her job, even temporarily. Worse, the effort involved in building a new practice was absorbing most of Dennis's time and energy, adding the primary responsibility for house and yard maintenance to Melanie's already heavy schedule.

"If we had had any brains, we would have stayed in an apartment for a couple of years until Dennis's practice got firmly established, then started our family. When I returned to work, we would have had two good incomes with which to finance a house. But the way we did it, we created an incredible economic and work load, and because Dennis had to concentrate on his practice to recoup some of our expenses, I had to carry most of the load by myself. By the time I turned thirty, I felt like the total drudge—work, work, work inside the house, outside the house, at the office. I think the house created more of a domestic double standard than a baby would have!"

Melanie was thirty-two before she felt she could afford to take time off from her job to have a baby, and even then, she gave the decision serious thought.

"Instead of the four children we had originally planned, I was wondering if I could possibly manage to care for one. All of a sudden, the road ahead looked endless, no light at the end of the tunnel. Dennis's profession had become, and would no doubt remain, a way of life for him, so everything else had become my job. He was earning relatively good money by that time, but the expenses of the practice continued to be heavy, and we still had years to go to pay off the loan. The house needed major repairs, and even the second car we had bought was getting old. I kept thinking, 'How did this happen? We've both worked so hard for so long—but when do I get my turn?' "

It was a question that many women were asking themselves as the financial realities of that decade eroded thousands of couples' good intentions to share fiscal and domestic responsibilities. Though many wives, like Melanie, were willing to work early in their marriages to contribute to the family's financial foundation, most found themselves compelled to do so—for the foreseeable future, not just for a year or two. Worse, again like Melanie, they found that the inexorable ticking of their biological clocks forced them to accommodate maternal duties right along with their full-time employment—a major snag in their original life plans. While they enjoyed the increased number and variety of work opportunities open to them, they resented the fact that employment was no longer a choice. It had become a necessity.

Even when financial circumstances were far more comfortable, a couple's great expectations could take a beating, it seems. Rosemary and Al are a good example. "I'm thirty-seven, and Al is thirty-six. We were both raised in the suburbs of Chicago," Rosemary begins. "We met in undergratuate school at Northern Illinois University, and we were married right after we graduated in 1970. At that time, I would not say I had any liberated leanings at all. I wanted to get married, and I wanted to work as a special education teacher, and neither of us was sure about having children. The women I knew were teachers, nurses, or mothers, and I really didn't challenge too much of what was going on."

Helping other people had always been very important to Rosemary, and teaching seemed to be the way for her to do that in those days. "The extremely bright and talented women were becoming lawyers or doctors, but they were exceptional. I was a bright student, but I wasn't number one in my class or anything. I would say I was pretty much the average college girl."

While Rosemary denies that her career aspirations were prompted by the fledgling women's movement of 1970, she admits that she was probably more career-oriented than others of that era. "I always wanted to work. I never had the idea of getting married and having someone support me. My mother had always worked as a nurse, and I didn't want to be taken care of in any sense. So in a way, I guess I was more liberated than I'm making myself out to be here. I wanted to be independent, and it was really important to me, when I graduated, to have a job and always to have a job, not to arrange my life around my husband's job."

What appealed to Rosemary most about Al, as opposed to other men she had dated before they met, she says, was his level of respect for women. "He didn't see me or any other woman as a sex object or someone who was lower in status to him. He really thought that I had a lot going for me, that I had a lot of potential. In fact, he's always been an optimist so far as my future is concerned, and he's been very supportive of everything I've ever really wanted to do."

Both Rosemary and Al attended graduate school after their marriage, though he went full-time and she part-time while working as a teacher to support them while Al finished his education. "Our relationship was very different then from what it is now. I can still remember calling him up and saying I was going to go someplace when I was finished teaching, and he'd say, 'Oh, come home. I'm lonely—I miss you.' He worked hard, but he had time to play golf or to spend with me once I got home from school, if I didn't have a class that night. So we had these two years while he was in graduate school that really weren't realistic, because Al had so much free time. It was very idealistic and romantic and wonderful. We had a lot of good times."

The division of household duties was a simple matter in those early days. Al did all the grocery shopping and maintained their two cars while Rosemary cleaned their one-bedroom apartment. Everything could be accomplished on a Saturday morning, and the work was equally divided. When Al accepted his first full-time position with an insurance company in Connecticut, however, things became quite different.

"When Al began an actuarial training program in 1972, it was a real adjustment. Even though we still had just an apartment to take care of, we didn't have much time together, and that was difficult. That was when I started to feel the pressures of growing up. As independent as I thought I was, I really wasn't. I needed a lot of his nurturing and time, but the program he was in was constant. He would work 45 to 50 hours a week on the job, and then he'd come home and work some more. When he wasn't working or studying, he'd be watching sports—so I went from having all that time together to having hardly any time together. I thought he didn't love me, but it was simply the reality of being married to somebody who was ambitious and who loved me just as much but had decided that this job was what he wanted to do."

Though it was difficult to adjust to her husband's new involvement with his career, the domestic double standard didn't really hit Rosemary until the couple bought a house. "When we had an apartment, there really weren't that many things to do, and they were fairly evenly divided. But when we bought a house in 1975, I found that most of the work involved in maintaining it fell to me, because all his time was taken up with working and studying for his actuarial exams." Still, Rosemary was able to temper her growing resentment by looking at things in perspective.

"I would say to myself, well, if he's studying for exams and working all day, then it's not such a big deal for me to do the cleaning. I looked at it time-wise. How much time was he devoting to a career that I would benifit from, too? If he gets to where he wants to go financially, and I do, too, through my work, it will all even out. We were both working equal amounts of time, though we were doing different kinds of things, so the domestic double standard bothered me, but not to the extent that it bothers me now."

After fourteen years of marriage, during which Rosemary successfully changed careers from children's special education to corporate management training and Al rose meteorically through the ranks to become one of the youngest executives in his company's history, the couple welcomed the arrival of a son in 1984. As wonderful as the baby has been, however, his birth served to underscore the existence of a double standard in the household. It was Rosemary's career, not Al's, that had to be interrupted for the baby to receive the kind of personal parental attention both felt was important for his well-being. It was she who got up nights because Al had to work at his demanding job the next morning. And it was she who bore the brunt of the planning and preparation, shopping, feeding, cleaning, laundry, day-care arrangements, and so on. Though she realizes that Al's career is as important to her financially as it is to him, Rosemary is eager for the day when both their lives will be more balanced, and the two have embarked on a five-year plan to bring them closer to that goal.

For hundreds of thousands of other 1970s couples, the fifty-fifty marriage model turned out to be as unrealistic and unworkable as the models which had preceded it in the 1950s and 1960s. Because of women's still limited earning power and career interruptions for childbearing; the employer's job market in which men were compelled to work harder and longer to improve or even to retain their status; and an inflationary economy that prohibited the hiring of any but essential day-care help, the domestic burden once shared equally between partners once again became woman's work.

What we had hoped would evolve into the New Marriage crumbled in the face of the New Reality. Working outside the home had become a necessity, not an option, for both partners in many cases; but largely because of the lingering disparity in the size of men's and women's paychecks, as well as the failure of employers to acknowledge their employee's needs for top quality, convenient day-care, the domestic double standard lived on.

No matter how many roles a woman juggles, whichever she performs within the confines of her residence are perceived as "not working." In this respect, the New Reality is the Old Reality reincarnate.

THE NEW REALITY

AS MY FRIEND SARA PUTS it, "The new reality . . . the assumption by women of at least two major roles, largely unaided by their male partners . . . is the old reality—in spades." The fact is that equal employment, without appropriate adjustments for the performance of essential, previously unpaid work done by women in the home, has resulted in each woman's assumption of dual and even triple full-time roles, and juggling them to her own and society's satisfaction is still viewed as her problem alone.

When the children lend a hand with household tasks, they think of it as "helping Mom out." When finances permit the hiring of paid help in the home, the husband views this as a charitable expenditure to "assist my wife." In short, the traditionally female responsibilities of home and hearth remain female, and the trade-offs and difficulties associated with fulfilling them along with those of a full-time job are still considered a woman's problem rather than one that every family member has a stake in resolving. Our liberated society has, in effect, created a wildly imbalanced new system of labor that penalizes women at home for every gain we have made at work.

Because this is true, many of us have found it necessary to restructure our lives to accommodate this inequity while pursuing, so far as humanly possible, our personal and professional goals. During a take-stock period in 1984, I examined the givens of my life: a husband willing to share domestic responsibilities but unable, because of his demanding and unpredictable job, to do so on any equal basis; children aged seven and eight who were becoming bored and restless in structured after-school day care; and the need for me to earn a substantial income. It was unrealistic to expect Wayne to abandon a satisfying career and an excellent early retirement program just to be home at 5:30 each weeknight, but we both wanted our kids to be able to expand the social aspects of their lives. By that time, I held a staff position as a corporate copywriter. Because, as a writer, I had the most professional flexibility, it became clear that it was up to me to work things out; and so, I decided not to renew any contracts that required me to work in clients' offices. Instead, I would accept only assignments that could be completed in my new home office.

What used to be our living room was converted into my new base of operations in March 1985 with the addition of track lighting, a large desk, file cabinets, and a computer table. Until we can afford to add a new room to the house, this is where I will complete my free-lance assignments and book manuscripts.

The creation of this new space pleased me enormously, heralding, as it did, the end of a rigid work schedule based on my clients' office hours. It was the beginning of a new era of flexible scheduling, determined by my personal and professional priorities. After years of scrambling, I felt I had finally succeeded in working out a more satisfactory alternative to the nine-to-five rat-race. Never again would I sit behind the wheel of the car in the driveway at 8:35 A.M., revving the engine while waiting for the school bus to collect the kids so I could tear through the suburban streets to meet a 9:00 A.M. deadline at a client's office. From now on, I could enjoy a second cup of coffee and the crossword puzzle while I kept an eye on the children waiting at the curb for the bus; and instead of a frantic commute, I would simply exchange robe and slippers for jeans and running shoes before strolling into my comfortable new office to begin work.

I expected a period of adjustment, of course, and there has been one. Working in isolation, no matter how comfortable, is very different from working amid friendly colleagues. I do miss that. Too, self-employment requires extraordinary discipline if one is to accomplish a good day's work when no one, after all, is watching. I also miss the conveniences of photocopier, sophisticated word-processing equipment, and well-stocked office supply cabinet; but in time, I will acquire these amenities. All in all, I feel I have done the right thing. Lots of people work out of their homes these days. It's one of the positive options of the new reality we have created for ourselves, and it's a wonderful way for women to combine working and mothering with a minimum amount of hassle.

Of course, there are still one or two little attitude problems to overcome. Not mine—other people's. May I tell you about my day? It's nearly nine o'clock on a Wednesday evening, but I have a point to make, so bear with me, please.

At 6:33 this morning, as I staggered from my bed to prepare breakfast for the children, I was intercepted by eight-year-old Jenna. I just barely stifled a yelp when I saw her, covered, as she was, with what looked like terminal poison ivy. I slathered her miserable body with Lanacort, administered a dose of antihistamine, and made a mental note to phone the school and the pediatrician at a more civilized hour.

After cooking, serving, and clearing up breakfast, I washed and dried my hair, waving a distracted goodbye to Wayne, who was off to Boston on business. Jumping into presentable slacks and a sweater, anticipating a visit to the doctor, I notified the school of Jenna's absence and began trying to reach the pediatrician. It being Wednesday, the traditional doctor's day off, my chances were slim, but I got lucky and reached Dr. Wolfson, who advised me to keep up the Lanacort and see if things got better or worse. I checked my son Ricky's school bag, brushed his hair, counted out lunch money, and sent him out to wait for the bus. By that time, Jenna's face was swollen so badly she could hardly get her eyes open, so I made another call to the doctor for an appointment, granted for 10:30.

During the next hour, I stripped all the beds in the house and collected towels, pajamas, robes, and yesterday's worn clothing and managed to wash, dry, and fold two loads of laundry between zooming around the upstairs with a vacuum cleaner and restoring both bathrooms to order. Getting Jenna into clean clothes was a trial, due to the inflamed state of her poor little hide, but we managed and went off to the doctor, who prescribed an ingestible cortisone. While the local pharmacist filled my order, I ran two doors down to the quick-print shop to copy a questionnaire I had prepared the night before for six interviewees in connection with a magazine article.

Cortisone tablets in hand, I drove Jenna to McDonald's, where I bought her a Happy Meal to compensate for her having to swallow six pills all at once. From there, we drove twenty-two miles to Simsbury, where I finally located the computer rental store with which I had arranged to lease a PC that was compatible with one of my new client's systems. They were short of help. Would I mind driving down the block to the warehouse and collecting the equipment myself? Locating the warehouse, I loaded—unaided—three sizeable cartons into the Datsun.

Twenty-two return miles to Newington later, I unloaded the same cartons and schlepped them into the living room where, I hoped, I would be able to figure out how to install the system without blowing it up. For the moment, however, other matters pressed. A client had mailed a request that I make airline reservations as quickly as possible for a June trade show. I tried. Three phone calls later, the best I could do was a 7:00 A.M. flight from Hartford on a Saturday morning. Yecchh.

A message on the answering machine informed me that my new coffee table, ordered months previously, had finally arrived but must be picked up by 5:00 P.M. Putting Jenna into the back seat of the car with a book and a pillow, I was off again, stopping at the grocery store for milk, bread, and cat food—the staples of our existence—and at the post office to purchase stamps and to mail the questionnaires I had miraculously remembered to staple together and address while I was trying to reach the airline reservation agent. At the furniture store, I discovered that the coffee table was too long to fit into the Datsun unless I could remember how to convert the back seat into extended storage space. I couldn't. Fortunately, Jenna could, and between us, we did. Cramming kid, pillow, groceries, and purse into the front passenger seat, I managed to get the coffee table into the car and head for home, barely skimming into the driveway before the school bus bearing Ricky arrived. It was 3:30, and I was exhausted.

After unloading the coffee table, preparing an after-school snack, and throwing a pound of ground meat into the toaster-oven to thaw (since I had forgotten to take it out of the freezer earlier), I took a cup of coffee with me into the living room to confront the computer components in their cartons. About the time I got everything unpacked and spread out on the rug, the nextdoor neighbors' children arrived to see what was new, engaging in much excited chatter about Jenna's poison ivy and the computer while I tried not to shriek. Eventually they moved into the family room.

After a frustrating half hour, I managed to get the computer connected to its keyboard and display unit but still had no clue as to how to access the new word-processing program, with which I was totally unfamiliar. Abandoning the struggle, I went to the kitchen to prepare dinner, which would be late. While the meatloaf and potatoes baked, I placed my every-other-day call to my mother, who lives alone. While we talked, I peeled and chopped vegetables for a salad. Hanging up, I remembered I had never finished the last load of wash and put the wet things into the dryer, then dashed upstairs to put clean sheets on two beds (Jenna's were still in the dryer) and toss clean underwear, shirts, and jeans into bureau drawers. I expected to encounter Georgie, the younger of our two cats, who customarily snoozes during the day in one or the other of the kids' rooms, but I couldn't remember having seen her since early morning, so I went outside to investigate. She was on the back deck, lying oddly on the cold flooring, and her only response to my love words was a dazed blink. When I picked her up, she howled frighteningly. It was 6:35 P.M., and the local veterinary clinic was closed.

I located the number of the metropolitan Hartford emergency veterinary service and called for directions. Collecting both children and scrawling a hasty note to Wayne, who had not yet returned from Boston, I put the cat in her carrier. Half an hour later, after several false turns in the dark streets of the city, I found the animal hospital, where we spent 45 depressing minutes awaiting the verdict amid the yelpings and mewlings of injured animals. The harrassed young doctor informed us that Georgie had been mauled, probably by an unaltered male cat, injected her with Amoxycillin and cleaned her wounds, handed me a bottle of liquid medication to administer for the next ten days, and requested forty-two dollars.

Returning home, I prepared a litter box for the cat, who must be kept indoors for at least three days, turned the oven back on, sent the kids to the bathtub, and folded the final load of laundry, which had sat so long in the dryer that it was wrinkled. I dished out the kids' supper, then trudged up the stairs one more time to put Jenna's sheets back on her bed. The message light on the telephone answering machine was blinking. An old friend who lives in Stratford, Connecticut, nearly eighty miles from Newington, had called with an invitation. "Why don't you take a run down here one afternoon next week," his recorded voice suggested cheerfully, "now that you're *not working*."

As I stood there with bed linen dangling and jaw sagging, it occurred to me, through my astonished outrage, that I had just been on the receiving end of one of the most infuriating clichés of womanhood: No matter how many roles a woman juggles, paid or unpaid, whichever she performs in the confines of her legal residence is perceived as "not working."

That's when I reached for the bourbon.

What does this mean? Why is work performed within the home so persistently undervalued? Is the answer as simple, and as horrifying, as because those who have traditionally done it—women—have done it not for money but for love? Or does it have something to do with the fact that those who are accustomed to having home chores done for them are irritatingly unacquainted with the skills and energies that doing such work well requires? I think the answer to both questions is "yes," and in these respects, the New Reality is the Old Reality reincarnate.

It seems clear that the women's movement, which began in earnest in the summer of 1970 when thousands of women marched down Fifth Avenue brandishing poster-paint demands for equal employment, educational, and political opportunities, has entered what Betty Friedan has so aptly termed "the second stage." Though it is true that the issues of the first stage, concerned largely with employment, are not entirely resolved, significant ground has been gained; and I concur with those who believe that the issues of the second stage center on the roles of men and women within the family framework. Having fought it out, toe-to-toe, in the workplace for almost two decades and having arrived at some basic understanding of each other's needs and rights there, we must now deal with the casualties of that prolonged conflict within our homes.

The price women have paid for improved employment

opportunities has included a loss of satisfaction within our traditional bailiwick, the household. Men, too, have paid dearly for their wives' career advancement, despite the family's new affluence, as jobs combined with domestic responsibilities sap more of both partners' energies every working day. She is torn between wanting her family to enjoy all the comforts of home—indeed, wanting to provide those comforts—and resenting her spouse and children, who expect her to provide them and to bring them home a regular paycheck, too. His notion of how a household ought to be run, by a stay-at-home wife and mother, is at variance with his genuine desire to support his wife's career aspirations.

These are conflicts that cannot be resolved effectively in political or legislative arenas. Our mutual role expectations must be reconsidered individually before they can be addressed collectively. Despite our weariness and resentment, we must confront the new reality and work out acceptable solutions to its problems one family—one woman—at a time. For quite a while now, I have been aware that this process has begun in my own family and in those of friends, relatives, and colleagues. The first phase consists of an acknowledgment of what the new reality is for today's working wife and mother.

A research report issued by the World Watch Institute in 1980 accurately predicted that equal job opportunity for women "will turn out to be a recipe for overwork" unless unpaid household labor is shared between men and women. Although nearly 50 percent of the world's adult women are in the labor force, the report continued, "they have retained an unwilling monopoly on unpaid labor at home. The result is a pronounced imbalance between male and female workloads, with unhappy consequences for women, men, and children."

Early in 1985 I attended my twentieth high-school reunion, a landmark experience I had anticipated with mixed feelings. From friends who had attended their twentieths, I had heard reports of a "Twilight-Zone," time-warp sensation brought on by the changed appearances and personalities of their former schoolmates. I was therefore delighted to find a banquet room buzzing with attractive, intelligent, articulate folks, most of whom seemed almost smug about the present state of their lives.

As I moved about the room, I was treated to glowing accounts of professional success, particularly by the women, who seemed just a bit too anxious to establish themselves as women who had "done something" with their lives. It was only after several hours of superficial chitchat that fatigue, and the open bar, loosened tongues sufficiently for the griping to begin, at which I felt the dismay of one who has unwittingly turned over a rock in the woods, exposing the crawlies beneath. Out it all came—the anger, frustration, and resentment of women who felt trapped by society's expectation that they tote that double-width barge.

"Where is it written," Angela, a corporate counsel, raged, "that everything to do with the children falls to me? They're Dom's kids, too, aren't they? But no matter what it is . . . a pediatric appointment, a parent/teacher conference at the school, shopping for new jeans and sneakers . . . is somehow my responsibility. Dom was very supportive when I decided to enter law school seven years ago, even though two of the kids weren't in school, but I'm convinced now that he thought the whole thing was just a passing fancy on my part. He never really thought I'd go through with it. The day I passed the bar, he as much as washed his hands of the kids. Now, either I do it myself, or I see that it gets done, which is usually even more trouble, while Dom comes and goes at will."

Angela's remark prompted a spate of similar complaints from the other women present. Justine, who returned to fund-raising work nearly a year ago, following the birth of her second child, described a typical day to me. "When I get home from work, I can't even look at the mail before I start getting dinner ready, because the kids are both clamoring to eat as soon as I pick them up at daycare. Since Doug doesn't even get home from his job until 6:30 most evenings, I have to feed the baby in his highchair while trying to coax my four-year-old son to swallow his vegetables instead of playing with them. My own dinner usually consists of what the kids don't finish from their plates. After that, there are the dishes to do, both kids to bathe, a story to read and the rest of the bedtime bit to get through. By then I'm ready to fall down, but there's a load of laundry to do for the next morning, the general clutter to deal with, and my own hair and clothes to get ready for the next day. If my mother or a friend has the bad luck to call at that time of night, she's likely to get her head snapped off," she admitted ruefully.

The hectic schedule doesn't let up once the work week is through, either, Justine pointed out, and we had to agree. "Even on the weekends—or maybe I should say, especially on the weekends—I'm doing something every minute I'm awake. It seems like I never stop moving, and they're all things that really have to get done, too. If I were two or three people, I might even enjoy doing most of them, but I just haven't got the energy to do my paid job as well as I would like to, be the best possible mother to my children, keep the house the way I think it should be kept, stay in touch with my friends, and give my husband a lot of attention. So, I always wind up shortchanging something and feeling incompetent and guilty." She laughs, chagrined. "Last week when I went to visit my mother on Sunday, I fell asleep on her. So what was the point of my making the effort to go over there at all?"

Cheryl, who is now a highly paid certified public accountant, as much as admitted that her determination to be both a mother and a professional person was threatening the survival of her marriage. "I'm tired of being Superwoman," she stated flatly. "I can manage the demands of my job. In fact, I love my job. I can even handle taking care of Missy," (her four-year-old daughter). "But I am totally fed up with being expected to keep the house spotless at all times, fall gleefully into bed with Rob whenever he feels like sex, and entertain his business clients with gourmet dinners as well. I've got clients of my own to entertain, and they've never received an invitation!

Something's got to go," she concluded ominously, and I had the distinct impression that Rob was about to become history.

Kirstin, a computer programmer for a large insurance company, confided that her husband was having a lot of trouble adjusting to the fact that she now makes a higher salary than he. "I think he's secretly glad, although he'd never admit it out loud, to know that he doesn't have to bear the entire burden of the family's support by himself. If anything ever happened to him, he knows I'd be able to support us just fine. On the other hand, he resents my success. When I was struggling along as a secretary and going to computer school at night, he was always helping out around the house. Now, he scarcely lifts a finger. I really think he wants me to fall on my face, to confirm his suspicion that it's all too much for me, so he can be the big, strong provider again."

The ambivalent feelings experienced by Kirstin's husband are an aspect of the new reality familiar to most husbands of working women. They are proud, on the one hand, of their wives' success in the business world and reassured by the extra paycheck in the family. On the other hand, their long-held ideas on how—and by whom—a household should be run are distinctly at odds with what they see occurring within their two-career homes.

An NBC News "White Paper" entitled, "Women, Work & Babies: Can America Cope?" which aired in March 1985, explored this conflict within the marriage of John and Tricia Blake of Delmar, California. The two had met and married while attending the same law school; and after ten years of marriage, they have two flourishing legal careers and daughters aged six and nine. In their law school days, John said, he was convinced that women, given the opportunity, could perform adequately the multiple roles of wife, mother, and professional. After they became parents, however, he changed his mind.

"Tricia comes in at the end of the day exhausted. Her days are full of conferences and clients. It's not that she's not trying hard to balance those roles or that she's not doing a very good job at what she's doing, given the time and energy constraints. But when you go out at 8:00 A.M. and come back at 5:00 P.M. after a day in the pressure cooker, it takes a toll on the other roles of life. Based on the way I grew up, I have this notion of how I would like to see the household function. I would like to see the kids more cared for by Mom. I would like to see the home more cared about by her. And I would like, simply, to have a lot more time together than we do."

Tricia, however, has no apologies, and in fact, she believes her daughters are fortunate to have her for a role model. "I've worked hard to be successful," she said. "I realize there is more stress and strain than I thought there was going to be, but I think it's manageable. Now the question is whether we have the maturity to work through this and to try to leave aside some of the strongly held emotional feelings that we have."

Opposing opinions on how things "should be" between partners undoubtedly are causing a great deal of tension in today's two-career marriages. Until our role expectations, for ourselves and our spouses, come closer to what is possible, in contrast to what each of us wishes were the case, there will continue to be much unresolved anger in our homes.

Like my former high-school classmates, many women are struggling futilely to be the very best wives, mothers, daughters, friends, and employees they can be simultaneously. Just sustaining all those roles at any level is extremely tiring, but striving to perform each equally well leads to feelings of guilt as well. "Fatigue" and "guilt" are words that crop up frequently in modern women's descriptions of their lives, defining the circumference of a vicious circle we have created through our impossible expectations of ourselves.

The mothers of young children who work outside their homes are especially prone to this unproductive syndrome, says psychologist Georgia Witkin-Lanoil, author of

The Female Stress Syndrome. "Women who work outside the home and also continue to work full time inside the home as caretakers of the family and household are often anxious and tired," she reports. Each of us may have high expectations of what we should accomplish on a given day, but those expectations must be tempered by an understanding of what is realistically possible if we are to avoid an unsatisfying, treadmill existence.

There are dismaying practical aspects to the new reality, too. The point of the women's movement was to improve women's choices in life; but to what extent has the choice of whether or not to work outside the home been eliminated? What might have been an extra paycheck ten or fifteen years ago, before the extraordinary inflation of the 1970s, has become the basis of economic survival for many families in the mid-1980s. Far from exercising an option to take paid employment, today's woman finds herself expected to contribute substantially to the family income, whether or not she chooses to do so, as well as to keep up with domestic responsibilities. Though her income is badly needed, she, by and large, continues to earn less than her husband, so her time on the job is perceived to be less valuable than his. Thus, when conflicts arise between her paid employment and household/family responsibilities, she is expected to put domestic duties first—but not to the point that, God forbid, she loses her job.

Because of this catch-22, women have engaged in a struggle to balance the demands of their multiple roles, exploring part-time work opportunities, job sharing, housework/child care pools, and other alternatives to carrying two or more full-time burdens. The fact is, many working women would prefer to remain at home with their infants and small children these days, but they can no longer afford to do so, either financially or in terms of job security and advancement.

Because their earnings are no longer superfluous, but are necessary to the family's financial security, even a two-month unpaid maternity leave from the job can make the budget uncomfortably tight. Women in fast-track professions also know that a decision to remain at home for more than a very few weeks following childbirth will brand them as uncommitted, less than serious about their work, and therefore undesirable prospects for promotion, regardless of the quality of their work.

In the early years of the women's movement, we assumed that our increased financial contribution to the family would be rewarded by a more balanced division of the domestic workload between partners, but this has not proved to be the case. To some extent, the double standard has fallen in the work place, but the domestic double standard remains firmly in evidence. According to family therapist and advisor Marjorie Shaevitz, the number of men who are actually sharing household responsibilities with their wives in any egalitarian way amounts to fewer than 13 percent in the United States. Society, she says, still acts as if the traditional family, with a stay-at-home mother, is the norm, which puts enormous pressure on working women to do it all or to maintain a facade behind which she struggles toward that unattainable goal.

Though society continues to regard motherhood as woman's highest calling, Americans' traditional respect for motherhood does not appear to extend to the workplace, in which working mothers are still not willingly accommodated. Consider these facts: The number of children under the age of six will increase by more than three million by the end of this decade. Yet, of about six million employers in the U.S., only about two thousand have any sort of program to help their employees meet their day-care needs. Further, there are presently more than thirty million working women of child-bearing age in this country, and statistics show that eventually most of them will become pregnant. Before they do, they should know that just becoming an expectant mother is likely to jeopardize their chances for promotion, and—more often than we would like to believe in this supposedly enlightened era—their jobs themselves.

And there are more penalties for motherhood in the

work place. The International Labor Organization reports that 102 countries around the world guarantee a woman her job back after childbirth, and 120 countries provide at least a partially paid maternity leave—but the United States is not among them. Three states have passed special pregnancy disability laws, which guarantee women their right to return to former paid positions following pregnancy—but those laws are already being challenged in court on the basis that they discriminate against men. One cannot help but feel that the United States would have adopted a national parental-leave policy long before now were the bearing of children a male biological function. Since it is not, the new reality is that most employers continue to regard maternity-related benefits as acts of beneficence to be doled out sparingly.

This, then, is the new reality; and I cannot imagine that there is a working mother over the age of thirty in this country who has not experienced several of its negative aspects, the bases of our growing weariness with having it all. Time and time again, we have presented reasonable, realistic proposals intended to ease the burdens—and improve the options—of bo h sexes, only to be turned back, as in the case of the Equal Rights Amendment, within inches of reaching our goals.

There have been moments of elation, of course—brief bursts of enlightenment and progress which cannot be denied; but for the most part, the women's movement has been a long, dispiriting confrontation on what history may well prove to have been the wrong battleground. Attitudes of mature individuals can be nearly impossible to reverse *en masse*, no matter how compelling the evidence; and the idea that the present generations of men raised in traditional homes will ever give more than lip service to a more egalitarian approach to domestic duties is probably ludicrous, no matter how often we point out what's in it for them.

We'll keep plugging away, of course; but to overcome this societal inertia, we must begin at the root of the problem—the rearing of both male and female children in this country—and establish new patterns and standards within our homes which will make the equal sharing of household and parental tasks perfectly natural to future generations. To do this, we must set aside, insofar as possible, our own fears and prejudices and anticipate the successful resolution of the issues still pending. By assuming, as individuals, that true equality in the home and in the work place will be the inevitable consequence of the evolutionary process in which we are engaged as a society, we can make it so—if not today, then tomorrow, certainly.

2

BRAVE BEGINNINGS

The women's movement has come full circle, returning to the domestic arena in which it began as we come to grips with the fact that attitudes cannot be legislated or otherwise forced into being. Instead, they must be nurtured by the examples set in the vast assortment of urban, suburban, and rural dwellings Americans call "home." Here, the most militant feminist and most ardent traditionalist can agree on a point or two, and here, we can help shape the futures of our sons and daughters who will build upon our brave beginnings.

The domestic double standard will not fall in the courts, the state legislatures, the Congress, until it falls in the home. It is within each individual family that we must declare war on the DDS by changing our approaches to family planning, household management, and child rearing.

Because the domestic double standard is a known factor in parenting, it is prudent for would-be parents to assess realistically what each partner's contribution will be after the baby arrives and to attempt to balance the parenthood equation in any way that works for them.

Planned Parenthood

It is Before Children, while the equitable division of household tasks is still relatively uncomplicated, that a couple has the best chance of mitigating the domestic double standard. The process is far more difficult once children are present; and so, if kids are on the drawing board, it is essential that today's young marrieds give themselves a chance to plan parenthood—to get to know each other well enough to predict with reasonable accuracy what life will be like once baby makes three, or more. Bearing in mind that the reality of a new baby may well blow the best-laid plan for shared parenting to blazes, it's still worth contriving one well in advance of a blessed event to set a "we're-in-this-together" precedent.

I like the new trend, in high schools across the country, of family-life courses in which adolescent boys and girls are paired in academic marriages, then confronted with a host of domestic situations to work through together. As a team, they plan monthly budgets and shop for bargains, consider the pros and cons of job offers and investments, decide how many children they will have and when to have them, explore home ownership and all that it entails, and generally cover the ground traversed by any newlywed couple, but without the emotional undercurrents of a mature love relationship.

While the exercise is not entirely realistic, it has many merits as a learning experience, focusing on the practical aspects of what is indisputably one of life's most complicated interpersonal relationships. After all, when learning to parachute from an airplane, you don't just strap on a chute and hurl yourself into midair, hoping you'll be able to overcome your fear of death long enough to pull the right cord. Learning how to be married—an infinitely more useful life skill—should not be a precipitous experience either, in which two frightened people struggle desperately to keep their mutual love and individual identities alive. When you learn the ropes in a low-risk atmosphere, you tend to be more confident in your ability to handle the real thing.

Had I and my contemporaries been encouraged to examine the practical aspects of domesticity more closely during our high school years, we might have spent far less time floundering in ill-fated relationships in the late 1960s and early 1970s. At the very least, we might more readily have accepted them for the short-term liaisons they obviously were. Still, we experimented in our own ways, groping in a decade of trial and error toward a clearer definition of what it was we wanted and needed in the men we ultimately married. It was the hard way to do it, admittedly, but few things worth having come easily. Even after we married, the great majority of us continued to swallow the Pill and to take things one day at a time in the hope of preventing our marriages from becoming casualties of the new war between men and women—the women's movement.

Despite the inevitable conflicts arising from women's struggle to redefine our futures, the 1970s were exciting years for us and for our newly enlightened male partners. While our vastly expanded opportunities were just a bit frightening, rather like having too large a menu from which to choose, they were unquestionably exhilarating. All things had become possible, for men and women both, and we reveled at our luck at having arrived at adulthood in time to participate in this brave new world as equals. "We've Only Just Begun" was the wedding song of choice; and having selected our mates for all the right reasons, we resolved to "start out walking and learn to run" toward the ideal modern relationship. It was, it turned out, a smart move.

Whether partners give themselves a year, five years, or even longer to explore this phase of their relationship, the time is well spent, for its importance to their future cannot be overestimated. It is during this period that they discover that they can or cannot live with each other's idiosyncrasies, find out how intrusive each other's friends and relatives will be, and gain insights into what their relationship will be once the sexual preoccupation has eased. Equally important in today's two-career marriages, they will confront each other's true expectations within the domestic arena and will begin the process of education, adjustment, and compromise necessary for them to work out a satisfactory division of responsibility for the future.

Married early in 1970, Wayne and I enjoyed almost six years as an unfettered couple before the birth of our son. Though we were hardly children on the date of our wedding at ages twenty-six and twenty-three, I think back on those early years as our adult childhood through which we romped deliciously. With little with which to concern ourselves except enjoying the salaries we earned from our as yet undemanding careers, we delighted in lunch-hour picnics in the park, spur-of-the-moment dinners at our favorite restaurants, and luxurious weeks in Florida, Bermuda, the Bahamas. We inspected every new house in central Connecticut, dreaming of the day we would own a home of our own; went into (and out of) business for ourselves in a small book shop; endured stormy episodes in our relationship with each other and our respective families; sampled new careers; and finally bought and furnished a small house in the suburbs of Hartford. And through it all we talked—more than two thousand days of conversation—and discovered that we were, and probably always would be, the very best of friends.

Whatever the future may bring, I will always cherish those years. Nothing can diminish the shine of those memories. They are there, the bedrock upon which our marriage has endured the difficulties of the ensuing years, and I could wish nothing better for contemporary newlyweds. Though the growing and constantly changing demands of two evolving careers, two children, and personal priorities may have damped the glow of our great expectations, we were able to deal with our new reality far more successfully, I believe, than we could have had we not had that important period of adjustment. Things did not work out exactly as we planned, but we learned a great deal about enjoying what is possible, if not perfect.

Some months back, while sorting out a carton of souvenirs from the early years of our marriage, I came across a contract I had composed and typed neatly on a single sheet of parchment on the occasion of our first anniversary. Complete with "Whereas" clauses and signature lines, this embarrassingly naïve document set forth the terms under which we would extend our partnership for another year. In 1971 those terms included the strict division of household duties, and I think we may actually have achieved that fifty-fifty arrangement for a while. On the whole, however, the document was far too rigidly black and white ever to survive in the gray area of domesticity.

Yet without those lovely first years of marriage during which I came to know in my soul that Wayne was a fair-minded, nonsexist man, I might easily have succumbed to the resentment that built steadily in me as his career moved sturdily forward and mine flagged, as he enjoyed the freedom to come and go and I scurried to accommodate his schedule. But because I was convinced beyond a shadow of a doubt that I had not married a sexist, no matter how insensitive to my needs he appeared to grow, I kept searching for the old Wayne under the layers of macho, and with patience and compromise, I found him again.

Because parenthood is often the circumstance which fully reveals the domestic double standard in a marriage, it is essential that the decision of whether to be or not to be parents be made on the solid knowledge of each other gained while playing house. Unfortunately, today's prospective parents are probably less aware of what having a baby in the family is really like than are the members of any previous generation. There were fewer young siblings in the families in which they were raised, and there is far too little education for parenthood present in standard curricula. Lamaze classes will get you through labor and delivery, but after that, you're pretty much on your own; and the realities of parenting can be overwhelming to couples accustomed to having their freedom as individuals and as partners.

Though parenthood has become a matter of conscious choice instead of the inevitable sequel to marriage, the fact of having to make such a momentous choice can be nerve-wracking in itself. It is not unusual for couples to dither over the decision for years as they attempt to assess, in advance of the event, their feelings about becoming parents and the ways in which their lives will be affected. Floundering amid conflicting statistics and opinions, their attempts to make good decisions can get bogged down to the point where they simply abandon the effort, stop practicing contraception, and let nature take its course. And eventually, for better or for worse, most become parents.

Without even delving into the current literature on the subject, which is extensive, or quoting the experts, who are numerous, after nearly twenty years of observing friends and colleagues and ten years as a parent, I can tell you in one sentence what couples really need to know about parenthood: Both partners' lives will be irrevocably altered by the experience—hers far more so than his.

Theories on why this continues to be so abound, and there is doubtless a grain of truth in each; but for whatever reason, and carefully worked out prenatal agreements on joint parenting aside, the primary responsibility for the rearing of children is borne by mothers. The specifics vary from family to family, but the bottom line remains the same.

Cartoonist Garry Trudeau, creator of *Doonesbury*, whose wife, NBC "Today Show" co-host Jane Pauley, bore twins in 1984, addressed this fact of married life characteristically during March 1985. Rick and Joanie, stock characters in Trudeau's syndicated commentary, had become the parents of baby Jeffrey, and Rick's editor, feeling there was a lot of interest in the modern, more involved, generation of fathers, asked Rick to keep a diary of his experiences. Trudeau acknowledged the disparities between motherhood and fatherhood via Rick's apparent oblivion to the same. "March 27. I notice tonight that I seem to have developed a special ritual with Jeffrey," read an entry in Rick's journal. "Every afternoon, Joanie picks Jeffrey up from daycare. They go to the park playground and then come home. Joanie reads to him, gives him a bath, and then after dinner, she brings him to me while I'm watching the news, and I kiss him good night. I do this every night without fail. It seems to work. Jeffrey's turning out great."

The following day's entry described Rick's return from work to find Joanie in tears, exhausted and demoralized from her struggles to pacify Jeffrey, who had thrown up all day and had not slept the previous night. Confidently, Rick assured her that they would survive this period in their son's life, would even laugh about it together one day. He then noted that he would be out of town on business for the ensuing three days and nights.

Fed up with Rick's superficial dabbling in parenthood, while she carried most of the load, Joanie frowned over Rick's shoulder one day as he waxed euphoric at the typewriter. ". . . and as I shake talcum on his tummy, I marvel at what a mystery he still is, what a miracle. All the work seems worth it today," he wrote. Finally, Joanie could contain herself no longer. "Rick, you know what would happen if those thoughts were written by a woman?" she snapped. "Nothing. Such a diary couldn't get published. From a woman, it'd be banal. But you're a man. You're not expected to think about any of that stuff! So you change one dirty diaper, and it's a literary event."

She stomped off, leaving Rick to ponder "The hard question: Have I been slumming?"

Trudeau's terse scenarios get right to the heart of the matter. Clearly, Rick genuinely wished to be an involved and supportive father and even believed that he was; but despite his good intentions, his first priority continued to be his job. He was a parent when it was convenient, while Joanie was a parent whether it was convenient or not—and always, always, she was *responsible* for the fulfillment of all parental responsibilities, whether or not she performed every task herself.

Whatever else a couple's decision about whether or not to be parents is based upon, this double standard must be acknowledged. Wishing that things were different—or that circumstances, attitudes, institutions, and national policies allowed them to be different—will not make it so. Obviously, we will continue to work toward that goal, but trust me, we ain't there yet.

Ralph LaRossa, associate professor of sociology at Georgia State University, shared some interesting observations on co-parenting in the October 1984 issue of *Redbook*. "The percentage of couples who share parenting in the truest sense of the word is minuscule, even among those who believe they have it all figured out in advance." LaRossa and his wife Maureen, who is a registered nurse and infant evaluator at Grady Memorial Hospital in Atlanta, are co-authors of *Transition to Parenthood: How Infants Change Families*. "It seems that wherever a couple starts on the continuum from traditional to modern expectations of parenthood, they end up more traditional than they were when they started."

The reason, LaRossa says, is that many couples attempt to conform to an ideal that may not reflect their personal values. For example, a couple may genuinely intend to share the care of their newborn, but once the honeymoon period of perhaps six weeks is over, old values begin to surface. The husband wishes to return to his evenings with the boys, and the wife is secretly relieved to be back in charge. Like a growing number of parents and professionals, however, LaRossa believes that co-parenting is an ideal worth working toward. The key to success may be the setting of specific, realistic goals—but as with most things, that's often easier said than done.

And so, modern couples can choose, within certain limitations, whether or not and when to bear children, but that persistent double standard mandates that women be prepared to deal with the consequences of those choices, most of which we cannot even imagine ahead of time, let alone plan for. The largely unchanged attitude of society toward working mothers versus its expectations of working fathers is one consequence that *can* be anticipated, however. Syndicated columnist Ellen Goodman, whom I enjoyed hearing address a "Women in Leadership" assembly in Hartford some years ago, summarized this syndrome neatly. When she returned to work after an absence for childrearing, she was apparently irritated repeatedly by well-meaning, but thoughtless, colleagues who demanded to know what she "did" with her offspring while she was at work. About the hundredth time this query was posed, she snapped, "Oh, I just leave them at home with the refrigerator door open, and it all works out," or words to that effect. Of course she had worked out appropriate child care arrangements! What on earth did people think? And why did no one ever direct that infuriating question to a working father?

Because the sun rises in the east, and women are the mothers, that's why. Far from designating the female half of a fifty-fifty partnership in parenthood, the term "mother" connotes an eighteen-year tenure as chief cook and bottle washer, nutritionist, guidance counselor, laundress, maid, chaffeuse, nurse, den mother, social secretary, hostess, and disciplinarian, whatever other roles (such as full-time professional worker) Mom may choose to add to the mix.

Intellectually, we may be able to accept these new responsibilities, but emotionally, we cannot predict our responses to them. For example, in 1984 more than half of all women with children under the age of six years were employed. Whether they work from necessity or by choice, these mothers share an extraordinary burden of guilt which is largely alien to modern fathers, despite their increased involvement with their children. Psychological studies on the effects of working mothers on child development abound, while no one bothers to question the effects of fathers' careers on their children. Fathers are still expected to work outside the home, and mothers considering doing the same are the targets of waves of unsolicited advice, pro and con. As a result, they feel guilty whatever they do. By staying at home for several years, they will be jeopardizing their families' financial security and burdening their husbands unduly with 100 percent of the responsibility for supporting their wives and children. By returning to work, they may irrevocably damage their children's psyches. Heads, they don't win; tails, they lose. Is there a way to make a good decision in advance?

Probably. Once a woman accepts the fact that she will be primarily responsible for the quality of the daily care her children receive, she can evaluate her chances of working things out fairly realistically; and if she does her best to evaluate her options, she will minimize her inevitable guilt, whatever she decides. However many unknowns enter into the parenthood decision, there are many aspects which are known, or can be investigated, before the Pill is banished to the wastebasket.

Regardless of her age or current employment status, every woman can answer two basic questions: Does she really want to be a mother? And does she really want to work—

or must she in order for the family to survive financially? The answers to these questions can go a long way toward making a good decision, since even the experts agree that what affects a child most is not whether a mother stays home or continues to work but whether she feels good about doing it. On the practical side, it is also possible to estimate the time and energy her husband will contribute to parenting, to explore and assess day-care options within the community, and to evaluate support systems that will be available to her if she chooses to, or must, return to work.

Indeed, the decision of whether or not to be parents centers around an exploration of options. If the available options are good, you can have reasonable confidence that you will be able to deal capably with unknowns that crop up later. And because the domestic double standard is a known factor in parenting, it is prudent for would-be mothers to assess realistically what their partners' contribution will be after the baby arrives and to attempt to balance the parenthood equation in any way that works for them.

As crucial as it is, "whether or not" is just one aspect of the parenthood decision. "How many" and "when" are equally important questions, though your answers may well need to be based on your experiences first time around. Another child is not, after all, simply a matter of stretching the food and clothing budgets a little farther. He or she represents a considerable investment of time, money, and most critical, a mother's emotional and physical energy. So how can you decide if once was enough? By considering the demands and rewards, the pros and cons, of your first mothering experience with the perspective of time—at least two years, say most mothers with whom I've spoken.

At a time when many women are compelled to work outside the home to help support the family, finances and time are important considerations as well. Since it is the woman who bears most of the child-rearing burden, even when she works full time, can she really afford to put herself in the double bind of having another child, both to care for and to help support? Will having a second baby jeopardize the delicate balance she has achieved between her work and maternal responsibilities?

A 1981 study of 1,600 American women explored this issue. Of those who said they wanted only one child, 33 percent cited financial reasons as the main ones for stopping there. They're good reasons. The costs of raising children are considerable. According to the Population Reference Bureau in Washington, D.C., the "direct maintenance cost" alone (out-of-pocket expenses such as food, clothing, and education, based on four years at a public university) was estimated at more than $85,000 in 1980, assuming a moderate standard of living. Added to that is the "opportunity cost," or the amount of earnings lost by the primary caretaker while she raises children instead of earning an income. Obviously, this varies according to each woman's rate of pay and the amount of time she takes off from the job to rear her children.

As startling as these figures are, they are overshadowed by this bold statistic: About 30 percent of a middle class family's annual income typically is spent on a first child. That's every year, mind you. The good news for those considering a second child is that Number Two will probably not be as costly as Number One. In fact, studies show that a second child costs only about half as much as a first or only child to raise to the age of eighteen, since the food budget can be stretched fairly economically and your present housing will most likely be sufficient. Hand-me-downs help, too, as baby cribs, high chairs, clothing, and toys are recycled thriftily. However, when you consider that 30% of your annual income is consumed by your first child, then add another 15% for your second child, the combined result of 45% of your annual income is an excellent reason to consider carefully the financial consequences of adding to your family. If you return to work after a second child's birth, you must also plan on a substantial day-care bill for two pre-schoolers for several years, since few sitters or centers give families with two or more children a significant break on fees.

Then there's the work involved. Based on a recent study, you can expect your first child to generate nearly 10,000 hours of extra housework from the time she is born until she graduates from high school, or about four years of full-time employment on top of your present work load! The same study indicates that a second child will create still another 3,700 hours of housework. The relative figures are quite similar, in fact, to the relative costs of rearing first and second children.

So it is clear that a second child means more expenses and more work than one child, but in the final analysis, only you can weigh these demands against your personal desire for another child. If you really enjoy your first child and think a second baby would be terrific, the trade-offs necessary to accommodate the needs of a larger family may well be worth it to you, but if your initial experience with motherhood doesn't turn out to be the pastel paradise you envisioned, you have every reason to limit your family to one child.

All of this advance planning for parenthood may seem rather far afield for two people who have "only just begun," but time has shown that the women who take the time to talk about the issues of parenting, to explore the division of domestic duties—in short, to play house with their husbands—are the ones who are ultimately the most successful at ameliorating the domestic double standard in their marriages. Creating and maintaining a satisfactory working partnership is an ongoing process, and wise adult couples will opt for a period of low-risk investigation—either by living together or by marrying and allowing themselves significant time in which to evolve as a couple—before adding children to the picture. Though many may disagree with this fail-safe approach to commitment, my feeling is that "playing house" is a valid phase in planned parenthood. It can't hurt, and it very often helps.

Having a strategy means putting yourself in charge instead of outside forces, agreeing on some goals and devising a plan to attain them through the effective use of resources.

HOUSEWORK: THE GREAT EQUALIZER

THE NICE THING ABOUT HOUSEWORK is that it's an equal opportunity job. Anyone can do it—and everyone should. While women may have accepted, for the time being, the responsibility for keeping the home fires burning, there is every justification for insisting that all who bask in their warmth help chop the wood and haul out the ashes on trash night.

A good housework strategy is arrived at collectively, with each family member buying into a long-range plan from which everyone will ultimately benefit. Devising a workable strategy involves accepting the givens of work/school/social schedules, then working with variables, such as abilities and preferences, within the overall framework of family priorities.

In our household, perhaps more so than in others, the division of labor is dictated by Wayne's work schedule, and I use the term loosely. The only thing we can count on is his absence from 8 A.M. to at least 6 P.M. Monday through Friday, and his presence at other times is only marginally predictable. That being a given for at least another eight years, until he is eligible to retire from

Federal service and engage in work over which he has more schedule control, I decided two years ago that if both of us were to continue working and our children were to have what we consider adequate parental supervision, it was up to me to create a "job" for myself that would give me the schedule flexibility Wayne lacks.

With that as my priority, I left my corporate copywriting position and set about building a free-lance business as a communications consultant. After a couple of false starts, I accomplished my goal, acquiring over an eighteen-month period a number of good accounts that I can service competently within the confines of the kids' school schedules. So from Monday through Friday, most weeks, I hold the fort—cooking the meals, doing the laundry, getting the kids off to school, and supervising their after-school activities in addition to putting in six hours a day on the job.

Because Wayne is fairly regularly at home on Saturdays, however, I consider this my main work day, during which I feel free to work for twelve gloriously uninterrupted hours, if necessary, on major assignments without worrying about domestic duties. And because Wayne gets four vacation weeks each year, he customarily uses two of them to cover the home base while I'm on semiannual business trips.

Having worked out a master schedule, the day-to-day grind is easier to manage, knowing that periodically I'll be relieved. Wayne, too, is relieved of guilt (fed by my continual carping about his work schedule), knowing that sooner or later he makes it possible for me to do my thing professionally.

Our rule of thumb is that whoever is home does whatever needs doing, from changing the sheets to taking the cat to the vet. When Wayne's working, he's working, and I don't call him to tell him the washing machine is on the fritz—I just get it fixed. And when I'm working, I expect the same freedom from domestic hassles, even if Jenna can't find her purple tights for dance class. Better they should run to Sears and get a new pair than to call Mom.

Over the years, however, the tasks that don't absolutely have to be done on a given day or at a fixed time have been divided between us largely on the basis of preference. I used to feel honor-bound to mow the lawn and shovel the snow from time to time to prove how nonsexist I was. But I really hate all yard work except gardening, while Wayne enjoys mowing and shoveling as a contrast to his sedentary job. So now I leave those tasks to him, assuming instead the indoor cleaning and cooking tasks that he most despises. While running the vacuum cleaner isn't my idea of heaven, it beats working up a sweat in the back yard. It's all in your perspective.

Ability also figures prominently in the overall strategy. Frankly, machinery intimidates me. I don't care what a car looks like as long as it runs, and when the dishwasher makes a funny noise, I'd just as soon buy another one as try to figure out what's wrong. Wayne, on the other hand, regards every ping and gronk as an exhilarating challenge and will contentedly dismantle and reassemble anything mechanical. He's beat the repair people out of a fat fee on more than a dozen occasions, too, so if he's home when it breaks, I'm happy to let him have a go. Otherwise, I just pick up the phone and call for professional help.

On the other hand, the prospect of Wayne figuring the monthly budget, writing the checks, or reconciling the bank statement is ludicrous. The man thinks that if you write it on the sheet headed "May Budget," the money will miraculously appear to cover it. Worse yet, he can't subtract accurately. The month I spent three hours cursing over an unreconcilable bank statement, finally tracking down three separate errors amounting to hundreds of dollars on entries he had made in the register, I took control of the checkbook, never to relinquish it.

Though their ability—and certainly, their interest—is severely limited at ages seven and nine, Jenna and Rick, too, get into the housework act. They eat good food, enjoy clean clothes and linens, and love our pet cats, but their appreciation of these things is regularly enhanced by knowing what having them involves. I can hardly expect them to do the laundry correctly, though that day will soon come; but I can and do expect them to help fold it and to put their things away neatly. They may not use the stove without an adult present, but they can and do help prepare meals—setting the table, making the salad, and practicing their cooking when I'm able to tolerate the inevitable mess. And when the cats, as cats will, leave dismembered mice on the back deck, the kids can darn well take their turns at the unpleasant task of clearing away the carcasses.

Involving the kids in household tasks is an important part of our overall strategy. Though it often seems easier to Wayne and me to do it ourselves rather than badger them into doing any kind of housework—and even then, let's face it, not very well—their understanding and accepting responsibility as members of a family is, we believe, an essential part of their total education. Housework should be shared by everyone who lives in a house. It is the great equalizer, keeping children, grownups, and in-betweens on a par in at least one arena. Nobody's a big shot when he's cleaning the toilet bowl, and a nine-year-old chef can take as much pride in his soup-and-sandwich lunch as I do in my beef stroganoff.

When it comes to the kids, though, patience is the key. At nine, Ricky thinks riding the tractor mower with Dad is a hoot, and the wobbly swath he cuts in the grass isn't really much help. But a few years hence, when we can turn him loose without fear that he'll chop off a foot, it will all be worth it, we hope. Jenna, too, is learning the ropes, and if as teenagers Rick prefers to cook and Jenna prefers yard duty, so be it. The point is, they'll each know how to do both, and more importantly, will know they're expected to pitch in as members of our family.

The fine points of housework strategy vary with the individual, depending as much on personal standards and pet peeves as on the ethics of family living. I have always envied friends and acquaintances with high clutter-threshholds, those contented individuals who can always find something more interesting to do than housework—and do it. Unfortunately I cannot function in the midst of chaos. I want the kitchen shears in the top left drawer in the kitchen, not in the family room being used to cut out paper dolls or on the basement work bench. I also want a pencil by each telephone, the plants to be watered and fed regularly, and the records put back in their dust jackets after use. It's a curse—I admit it, but that's who I am. Happily, I married a man similarly addicted to neatness, for which I will always be grateful to my mother-in-law.

As a result, our house is almost always presentable. Despite our crazy schedules, tidiness, undergirded with cleanliness, is a Sprankle priority. Though we don't carry it quite as far as a former neighbor, who mowed her lawn twice a week and washed every window and screen monthly, we do have neat-freak reputations. Still, some things are beyond even my comprehension.

The sight of a full laundry bin might drive me to distraction, but I was heartily amused when a colleague confessed that she could not break herself of the habit of removing laundered items one at a time from the washing machine and shaking them out before placing them in the dryer. "Now, that's really going too far," I laughed, only to be outvoted by several other members of the office staff who staunchly asserted they did the very same thing. Though I still think it's a waste of time, since everything gets tangled up again in the dryer anyway, I've learned to keep my mouth shut in public about such things, especially since I was hooted out of a room when I confided to a group of working mothers that I washed the wastebaskets regularly.

Everyone has their little quirks, it seems. To my knowledge, I have never vacuumed the inside of a lampshade, but I know people who do it weekly. I can let the windows go for a year, but every floor in the house gets vacuumed, mopped, and waxed frequently—probably because we usually go unshod indoors and any dirt or grit makes itself felt. Most houses I visit have comfortable stacks of magazines, newspapers, mail, bills, and other domestic flotsam piled here and there, and it doesn't bother me one whit; but at our house, magazines have a life expectancy of about a week, and the newspapers and junk mail are consigned to the trash daily.

Managing the continual ebb and flow of possessions is a sore point in many households, as some family members tend to be pack rats while the clutter drives others mad. I am never happier than when I am moving things out of the house—outgrown clothes to the Salvation Army bin, unused toys to the local day-care center, bottles and newspapers to the recycling center, paperbacks and puzzles to the library book-sale. Wayne and the children, however, can get sentimentally attached to any inanimate object that stays around for more than a week, so I wage a constant uphill battle against their reluctance to part with even the most disreputable of their precious possessions.

Another step in my personal housework strategy was a bit tougher to take: identifying specific tasks to get outside help for, then employing people who would perform them satisfactorily. The trouble with being a neat freak is that you resist hiring outside help because you always feel it will be better and quicker if you do it yourself. I certainly felt that way for years, but I've had to force myself not to be quite such a housework elitist. The demands on my time became such that I could not personally attend to every domestic detail and give adequate attention to my family, my clients, and myself. So, something had to go. What would it be?

My objectives in hiring help were to get rid of some of the housework burden while receiving full value for the money we'd have to expend. Considered in this light, hiring someone to do routine weekly cleaning seemed unsatisfactory. As anyone with young children will verify, the once-a-week theory of housecleaning is laughable. Half an hour after the housekeeper leaves, all that expensive dusting and straightening can be destroyed by two kids and their playmates, who have emptied the toy chests in the family room, trailed through the house munching on a plate of crackers, shampooed a doll's hair in the bathroom sink, and changed into dry clothes, leaving the discards where they fall. A clean kitchen lasts maybe half that time, what with four people satisfying healthy appetites and creating crumbs, milk-rimmed glasses, and a grease-spattered stove in the blink of an eye. No, I had no intention of paying out forty dollars or more a week to support this kind of futile effort. I would continue the daily rounds myself.

There were, however, tasks with longer-lasting results that I would gladly pay to remove from my agenda. The first that sprang to mind was window-washing, a chore I loathe both for its tedium and its seeming endlessness. I always get too bored to clean more than two or three windows at a stretch, and having stopped, can usually find excuses not to get back to the job for weeks. How delightful it would be to have someone else take over, but who would wash my windows as meticulously as I?

A young man who had specialized in cleaning windows and floors for more than ten years, it turned out. Assuming I had contacted a college student who washed windows for pocket money, I expected to find a gum-snapping youth carrying a boom box at my door. Instead, I was impressed when a sturdy twenty-eight-year-old turned up promptly at the appointed hour with a two-man crew and a van full of professional-looking equipment. My doubts about the quality of work they would do vanished when the boss man surveyed the house briefly, assured me that no mere homeowner could achieve the results that he did, and set up an assembly-line process that would have impressed the corporate executives at IBM.

Ninety minutes and sixty-three dollars later, the crew stowed pails, ladders, and squeegies neatly in the van and disappeared, leaving me dazzled by a houseful of gleaming casements, storm windows, and screens. Even the fanlight on the front door and the garage windows, which I had managed to ignore for years, glistened. I promptly budgeted professional window-cleaning twice a year and have never looked back. It's still amazing how much I enjoy knowing I'll never have to wrestle a recalcitrant storm window from its grimy track again.

Having acknowledged that there were tasks even I could not do as well as maintenance professionals, with their industrial-strength chemicals and specialized equipment, I selected a second major—and dreaded—seasonal chore to hire professionals to do: steam-cleaning the rugs and carpets. Previously, I had rented equipment and spent two dismal days a year on this drudgery, but I now resolved to cross this off my list as well. After making a few calls and comparing prices, I contracted with a local establishment that specialized in cleaning draperies and floor coverings. When one slightly built, sixtyish gentleman showed up, I again experienced momentary doubt, but I was delighted with the results. Three hours later I smiled upon hundreds of square feet of damply glowing carpeting. Even the motor oil tracked in by the kids using the garage entrance had vanished from the hall rug, and I was happily reacquainted with its original color. This, too, was obviously well worth the $100 it cost.

Following these two eminently successful trial runs, my enthusiasm for professional maintenance was tempered only by my budget, which remained limited. Still, by weighing costs against the improved quality of the results, as compared with my amateur efforts, I eventually added a yearly cleaning for the upholstered furniture and an annual washing down of walls and woodwork to the household budget. I even purchased a discount ticket book for the local car wash, though I still like to get out the hose and the suds and spritz off the Datsun on a hot afternoon.

The total cost of these services is just $500 a year, an expenditure that seems paltry in contrast to the peace of mind I derive from it. Knowing that these back-breakers will be well and regularly accomplished without me makes running the vacuum cleaner and mopping out the bathrooms seem mere child's play.

* * *

To me, having a strategy means putting yourself in charge instead of leaving things to outside forces, agreeing on some goals with the other members of your family, and devising a plan to attain them through the effective use of internal and external resources. Arriving at that plan is a highly personal process, but I've discovered that the great majority of working mothers have one.

Cassie MacNamara, for example—an executive secretary of my acquaintance whom I've long admired—has an entirely different, but equally effective, housework strategy. The mother of nine children (two sets of twins!), Cassie has worked outside her home for more than twenty years, a feat of which I stand in awe. How, I once wondered out loud to her, does she manage a full-time job and an eleven-member household without losing her sanity?

Through delegation and teamwork, she responded without hesitation. Each family member, from her twenty-year-old daughter to the seven-year-old twins, is responsible for cleaning their own rooms as well as the bathrooms they share, for depositing sheets, clothing, and towels into the laundry bins on Saturday morning, and for returning them to beds, racks, and bureau drawers on Saturday evening. In addition, each older child is responsible for getting one younger child ready for school each weekday morning. Everyone clears his or her own dishes from the table at the end of each meal, rinsing and stacking them in the dishwasher, and takes a turn at emptying the machine at the end of its cycle. While Cassie takes responsibility for grocery shopping and most of the cooking, she is always aided by at least two of her brood in these tasks, depending on who's around. And every three months, the entire family rallies for a top-to-bottom shakedown of the rambling colonial they inhabit, with assignments ranging from trimming the houseplants to regrouting the bathtubs. "No problem," she smiled, and I retreated to marvel at her managerial talents.

Those who are unbothered by daily clutter have an entirely different perspective on housework. I first observed this in the person of my Katherine Gibbs roommate Joanne, who was personally fastidious, yet totally unconcerned about the chaos she created around her. When she wanted to retire for the night, she just shifted the pile of clothes and books from her bed to her desk, reversing the process each morning when she arose. She never intruded on my space, never lost anything, and never had an eyelash out of place. It was simply that to Joanne, housework on a daily basis was a waste of time and energy. A couple of times during the year she accommodated her personal standard of cleanliness by hurling every shoe, book, and curler into the dormitory hall, energetically vacuuming and washing down every nook and cranny of room and closet, then replacing her belongings in their original stacks—and that was that.

What worked for Joanne seems to work for others in my circle of friends as well. Having been secretly critical of a neighbor's sloppy domain for some months, I was amazed one bright spring morning to see Sandy's husband and children methodically emptying the house into the back yard. Room by room, the contents of their home moved outward through the kitchen door, while Sandy disappeared in the family station wagon. An hour later, she returned to unload steam-cleaning equipment, window washing gear, and boxes of solvents and soaps.

By 5:00 P.M., following an eight-hour marathon of scrubbing and reassembly, her husband was on his way back to the rental shop while Sandy serenely lit the charcoal for a backyard barbecue and played badminton with the kids. Every year the ritual is repeated, spring and fall. As long as it's clean underneath, Sandy shrugs, who cares about a little surface clutter?

Who, indeed? Though it is anathema to me, clutter seems to be the very breath of life to some women. A copywriter with whom I once worked at a major corporation had a desk that epitomized clutter, with every surface and drawer clogged with print samples, office supplies, and personal possessions of every description. Framed photographs of her daughter teetered precariously atop stacks of slippery press kits, while tangled clumps of paper clips and elastic bands vied for space with packets of Sweet'n'Low, half-completed crossword puzzles, and hundreds of scraps of paper—all scribbled upon—in her center desk drawer. Until Marcie became ill, in fact, no one had ever dared to open any of the other drawers in that infamous desk for fear we'd never be able to get them shut again. When she was forced to take an extended leave of absence, however, a temporary copywriter was hired to fill in, and it fell to me to clean out Marcie's desk for the new worker.

Once the initial shock wore off, I rather enjoyed sorting out the unspeakable jumble into neatly labeled cartons, which would await Marcie's return. How nice it would be for her, I thought charitably, to return to the order I had created among her things. Her reaction, however, was less than ecstatic. In fact, I seriously thought she might faint. "My God!" she blurted in genuine distress. "You didn't throw anything *out,* did you?"

Somewhat taken aback, I assured her that I had not, but only packed her possessions away in cartons. The color returned slowly to her face. To Marcie, the clutter that makes me crazy is a link to sanity—tangible evidence of the past and present that makes an uncertain future manageable. The constant, reassuring presence of completed professional assignments, former associates' telephone numbers, family mementos, old appointment books, cancelled checks, and other miscellany provided a stable base from which to proceed with the day's work, and I had rocked her very foundation by disturbing her precious cache. Everything Marcie needed in order to function was either on or in that desk, and while nobody else could find anything there, she could do it every time, at a moment's notice.

From Marcie, I learned a valuable lesson in humility: If it works for someone else, butt out. Not everyone is inherently tidy—and there's a reason they call people like me neat *freaks,* after all. And so, when my kids return from friends' houses making high-handed remarks about untidy bedrooms and kitchens, I make it a point to tell them to mind their own business, that people have a right to live the way they want to under their own roofs. When I catch myself sneering inwardly at the housekeeping standards of my own friends, I similarly nip it in the bud. Doing it right doesn't mean doing it my way. It just means doing what works for you and your family.

It's the "and your family" part of that last observation that is usually the stumbling block in devising a housework strategy. Even people who are blood relations don't have the same standards and needs in terms of their indoor environments, and when these are radically different, conflicts invariably arise.

As it happens, Wayne, Rick, and I share a need for order, but eight-year-old Jenna is the family maverick. If her clean clothes make it to her room, they have been properly put away, in her view, even though they remain piled on a chair. When she changes from her school clothes to play togs, the discarded items remain where they land on the floor. She moves through her days leaving a trail of toys, books, crayons, socks, towels, banana peels, and what have you in her wake, totally oblivious to disorder. A sweet and obliging child by nature, she would be glad, I think, to accommodate the rest of us by keeping closer track of her belongings, if it ever occurred to her. The problem is, it doesn't until her father or I demand, in ever louder tones, that she do so.

Our thousands of exhortations, over the years, to "pick it up and put it *away*" have instilled not one iota of orderliness in Jenna, who can return from school five days running having left something fairly essential behind. Just a few weeks ago, she got off the school bus wearing only one shoe. Don't ask me how that's possible. All I know is that the child managed to lose a shoe while wearing it and wasn't sufficiently bothered by the loss to notice it. My best guess is that she finds what's going on inside her own head and among her friends, to whom she is genuinely devoted, so much more interesting than inanimate objects that she simply hasn't much awareness of "things." Her perception of her environment is obviously quite different than most people's. Going into her room one evening recently to tuck her in, I looked around in disgust and said, "This room is a slum, Jenna!" Her gaze followed mine to the discarded clothing on the couch, the toys spilled out of her pine chest, the disassembled dollhouse on her desk, and the jumble of dusty books and records on the floor by her bed. "Gee, Mommy," she said with real surprise, "I don't see it that way." And I guess she really doesn't.

So, if that's the way Jenna is, how far can we justifiably go in imposing our standards on her? It's a question with which I've wrestled for some time now. Though it involves a certain amount of stoicism on my part, I've concluded that she must arrive at her own standards for her own space, but she must also abide by ours when it comes to the rest of the house. Personal hygiene isn't a problem, since she loves to bathe each evening and revels in clean clothes and bedding. Anything that smells bad to her is "Yuck!", so that puts the kabosh on total slovenliness. Beyond that, I simply insist that she not annoy the rest of the family with her sloppiness, collecting her scattered belongings at the end of each day. Further, any item I put on the stairs for her to carry up with her that's still there after she's gone to bed goes into a carton in the garage for six months, a rigidly enforced rule that seems to carry some weight.

Conflicting standards between adults and children are one thing. A similar conflict between spouses constitutes a far greater problem in creating a housework strategy, however. Not only is there continual friction between partners with which to deal, but the problem of setting standards for the kids is exacerbated. Without a unified front, household rules are tough to enforce, and the domestic double standard is even more than usually evident.

Not having this particular problem in my family, I turned to friends for helpful suggestions and discovered approaches ranging from grudging acceptance to good-humored practicality. Bettina, whose husband enjoyed twenty-two years of round-the-clock maid service from his mother and three sisters before his marriage, has decided to place domestic harmony above a tidy house, for the most part. She knew, she says, what she was getting into when she married Bill, whose idea of helping around the house is rinsing out his empty beer cans before leaving them on the kitchen counter. After years of bickering about his habits, she has called a permanent truce, allocating to Bill only those tasks she has noted he does by preference anyway.

While he can't seem to get the hang of putting his dirty socks in the hamper, Bill is a model of competence at the supermarket, comparing unit prices with mathematical precision and selecting only the freshest, firmest produce. So Bettina deals with laundry, and Bill does the shopping. A spider could spin a web in the middle of the living room without Bill's noticing, she maintains, but a dandelion in the front lawn stops him dead in his tracks. So Bettina vacuums and dusts, and Bill mows and weeds.

Far from being confused about their parents' conflicting standards on housework, Bettina maintains, the couple's two sons seem to be absorbing the best of both, following her lead inside the house and accepting instruction from Bill on grocery shopping and yard work. Though only ten and twelve, she confides proudly, her sons never miss a good coupon in the Sunday newspaper, and ChemLawn couldn't improve their manicured half acre.

Though Bettina has found a workable strategy for dealing with the domestic double standard she inherited from her inlaws, not every woman is so successful. The worst scenario seems to be that in which Mom lacks even moral support from Dad on household matters, forcing her into the unpleasant role of "heavy" to enforce the standards she feels are right for her family.

My neighbor Maggie had this problem. "Sometimes I heard myself screeching at Ted and the kids about expecting me to do everything for them, and I felt like the Wicked Witch," she moaned in response to my query, "and that was probably worse than just shutting up and doing it all myself." She would probably have done just that, she says, if she hadn't taken it upon herself to instill some sense of domestic responsibility in her son and daughter, both in their early teens. Besides, she admits, their unrealistic expectations were largely her own doing.

Because she stayed at home for nearly ten years following the birth of her children, 16 months apart, Maggie just assumed that running the house was her business, freeing Ted and the children to concentrate on job and school responsibilities. She realized too late, when she returned to full-time employment, that it was a tough position to reverse.

"Ted always made a good living from the hardware store, and I hadn't enjoyed office work very much before we were married, so when the kids came along, I decided to concentrate on homemaking. By staying at home, I probably contributed as much to the family budget as I would have by working, after deducting the cost of day-care for two small children. I taught myself how to paint, wallpaper, and do minor household repairs, and we got all our supplies at cost from the store. I clipped coupons religiously, followed the clothing sales, and even learned how to cut the kids' hair. But a couple of years ago, I took a hard look at our savings account and realized there was no way Rob and Melanie could go to college unless I started making money, not just saving it. So I brushed up my clerical skills and found myself a job."

The demands of full-time employment were greater than Maggie had anticipated, however, and she soon acknowledged that she needed help from Ted and the children. Accustomed to her selfless ministrations for more than a decade, they were shocked at her new expectations and resisted the tasks she attempted to delegate to them. After a year of unproductive bickering, Maggie finally decided to confront her family with the economic facts of life.

First, she spent several evenings compiling a record of how she had managed to run the household on a single paycheck in previous years, since the family budget was another task Ted was happy to let Maggie handle. Next, she researched the Consumer Price and Higher Education Price indices for the past ten years at the local library. Armed with this information, she sat Ted, Rob, and Melanie down at the kitchen table after dinner one night and calmly laid it all out for them. If Rob and Melanie wished to finance their college educations themselves, she said, she would be only too happy to resign her office job and continue to take care of things at home. If they expected her financial help, however, they would simply have to pitch in.

Her matter-of-fact presentation of the alternatives had the desired effect. Even Ted was stunned, she now recalls with amusement, and her family's attitude has changed drastically since that memorable evening. Before they left the table, Ted had masterminded a plan for domestic operations, as he called it, posting it on the refrigerator door. No longer is Maggie expected to bring home the bacon and cook it as well. Rob has assumed kitchen duty, proving to be a deft baker as well as chief cook and bottle washer, while Melanie charges energetically through the major cleaning chores on Saturday, when Maggie shops for groceries and runs errands. For his part, Ted attends to the laundry and the bill-paying, chagrined at his ignorance of household finances in past years. Under his watchful eye, the savings account on which Rob and Melanie's college education depends has burgeoned, and every member of the family takes pride in their family effort.

As is the case in most negotiations, getting everyone to buy into a long-range plan to achieve mutually rewarding objectives is central to developing a good housework strategy, and it's never too early—or too late—to work one out. The Little Red Hen made a charming story, but if you ask me, she waited far too long to tell her barnyard cohorts to shape up. Suffering in resentful silence is an invitation to an ulcer, and continual quarreling is merely exhausting. As Maggie so ably demonstrated, one evening's calm communication is worth years of emotional shouting matches.

As soon as the kids are old enough to understand the concept of sharing, they're ready to get in on the act; and if women ever hope to banish the domestic double standard, we must orchestrate the performance, not continue to play all the instruments. It doesn't really matter, in the end, who does what. What does matter is that everyone shares the total load—sequentially or concurrently, but so far as possible, equally.

By including our children in the give-and-take of every aspect of family life, we can spare them much of the floundering so many of us have had to do to achieve an appropriate balance and go a long way toward laying the domestic double standard to rest in future generations.

SETTING THE KIDS STRAIGHT

IN A FOURTH-GRADE CLASS in California, both boys and girls are exposed to the fun and difficulties of caring for a small child. In middle and high schools in Connecticut, adolescents are paired in paper marriages and shown the ropes of household management, including such skills as budgeting, shopping, investing, and family planning. Programs like these encourage more sharing in all aspects of future marriages, but such training, to be truly effective, cannot be confined to the classroom. To ensure that tomorrow's moms and dads will form egalitarian partnerships, today's parents must make a concerted effort to overcome their own prejudices and raise their children differently from how they themselves were reared.

Ideally, both partners will be committed to this facet of their children's upbringing, since a united parental effort is always more significant in children's minds than one in which the principals are at odds. In this I've been fortunate, since Wayne is as open as I to the idea of our son and daughter sharing in the spectrum of domestic duties. Because I was one of two daughters, it is not surprising that my sister and I picked up a lot of traditionally male skills, learning to mow the lawn, shovel the snow, and rewire the lamps right along with our lessons in cooking, cleaning, and sewing; but Wayne had three sisters as well as a brother, which makes it rather remarkable that he is as well acquainted with the business end of a vacuum cleaner as he is with a skill saw. To my mother-in-law Louise, work was work, indoors and out, and every member of her household pitched in.

The problem goes way beyond changing the attitudes of less enlightened husbands, however. It is even more imperative that we mold the attitudes of tomorrow's husbands—and wives—in ways that will cause the domestic double standard to crumble once and for all. We've got to set the kids straight, and that means getting ourselves straight first.

In *The Girl I Left Behind,* author Jane O'Reilly says the real root of the problem is that "even as parents discover themselves turning into their own parents, they discover that their children are growing up to be like themselves. Most parents hoped that their children would be different, and, of course, better. Instead, the children turn out, most of the time, to be no better than could have been expected." It is extraordinarily difficult, O'Reilly says, to accept in a child what you have always hated in yourself, so we develop convenient blind spots about our own least favorite personal characteristics. "Mona tells me she can't bear her daughter's slovenly habits. I have known Mona for twenty years, and she has never hung up her clothes. She throws them on the bottom of the closet. Greg's father complains that the boy will never get into Harvard Law School if he doesn't cure his obsessive compulsion to rebuild bicycles. Greg is fifteen, and his father hated Harvard Law School, hates being a lawyer, and is happy only when rebuilding boats."

I, too, often chuckled over similar observations made by the parents of my children's friends until I came smack up against a blind spot of my own. As a child, I hated it when my mother berated me for waiting to be assigned a task instead of just noticing that it needed doing and doing it on my own. "You've got eyes," she would point out time and time again. "Use them! If the trash basket is overflowing, you don't need me to tell you to empty it." Unfortunately, though, I did need her to tell me. Kids always do, and they always resent having their lack of household initiative nastily remarked upon. That's why it came as something of a shock to hear myself dressing down Rick the other evening on the very same subject.

"You kids do nothing around here," I snarled quite unfairly, since both children keep their own beds made, rooms straightened, and dishes cleared away on a daily basis and are usually reasonably willing to help out around the house when I ask them to do something specific.

"But I don't know what to do," Rick protested. "You always do everything, so I'm not sure what needs doing. Why don't you just tell me?"

"I shouldn't have to tell you," I heard myself saying in a voice alarmingly reminiscent of my mother. "You've got eyes! You can recognize a full wastebasket when you see one, and you know it's Monday and the trash has to go out to the curb."

"No, I don't know that," he persisted. "I don't know which night is trash night because it changes whenever there's a holiday. So why can't you just tell me?"

Oh, Lord, I thought in frustration. The more things change, the more they stay the same. How do you instill a sense of initiative in a kid about something as uninteresting as housework? I gave the matter some thought over the next couple of days and concluded there could be no initiative unless there was freedom to exercise it, and there was little satisfaction to be gained by carrying out a mundane chore that has been assigned by one's sarcastic female parent. Therefore, the kids needed to know what they might productively do on their own at any time without interfering with an established routine or being redundant. I drew up a short list headed "Things You Can Do At Any Time To Help," and posted it on the refrigerator door. Each task was chosen on the basis of the length of time it would take to complete (little) and the amount of supervision it would require to get done to my satisfaction (none). The tasks were emptying all the upstairs wastebaskets into the kitchen trash can, setting the table for whatever meal came next, unloading the dishwasher, folding a load of clothes from the dryer, straightening out the toy cupboards in the family room, sweeping the front porch, cleaning the bathroom sinks, and refilling the cats' food dishes when empty. I posted the list without comment and awaited developments.

The next evening, Rick mentioned ever so casually that he'd reorganized the toy cupboards, if I cared to come see. "Thanks, Honey," I said after surveying his arrangement briefly. "I like the way you put all the box games together." As I kissed his cheek, Jenna bristled jealously. When she came downstairs after her bath, she was toting the wastebasket from her room, into which she had emptied the upstairs bathroom baskets, as well. "I used mine to collect in because it's the biggest," she announced importantly.

"Good idea," I agreed and pinched her bottom fondly. She giggled her way back upstairs while I smirked behind my newspaper. So far, so good. The next afternoon, I came upon her struggling with our recalcitrant can opener, the cats' dishes beside her, and I showed her how to lean on the lever for maximum effect. When I returned to the kitchen later to make supper, I found that Rick had set the table. Again, I commented briefly but appreciatively, then offered the information that the blade of the knife always gets turned toward the plate. And so on.

The novelty will undoubtedly wear off, and I will once again be compelled to ask the kids to do this or that, but all of us have learned something, I think. The kids have learned that it's satisfying to feel they are able to do certain things as well as the adults in their house and that appreciative kisses and pinches beat the hell out of parental recriminations, while I've discovered that you can catch more flies with sugar than you can with vinegar every time.

Getting the kids to buy into the concept of sharing household tasks at the ages of eight and nine is difficult, since their abilities, at this point, are distinctly unequal to Wayne's and mine, so we try to base their participation on time as well as on skill. Obviously, we spend far more time than the children do keeping up the house and yard, but there are occasions on which the equal time concept can be used very effectively. A friend of mine suggested that I try the "big payoff" approach she often uses with her kids, usually on a weekend when everyone has something they'd much rather be doing than housework. "It will be a beautiful Saturday morning, and the kids are itchy to get outside with their friends or to go for a bike ride, and Allan and I want to play some tennis. But the laundry is spilling out of the bin, and the house is a mess, so we make a deal. Everyone spends exactly one hour on the house, and then we can all do whatever we want for the rest of the day. I set the egg timer for sixty minutes, and the race is on."

It's amazing, she says, how much gets done in one energetic family hour. In fact, it has the flavor of a friendly competition, with much good-humored comparison of who has accomplished what as the dustrags and soapsuds fly. Though it's impossible to hurry the inexorable cycles of clothes washer and dryer, her teenage son, on one memorable occasion, grabbed every scrap of laundry in the house and rushed to a nearby laundromat where he successfully washed and dried five loads in one hour by shortening the time setting on five washers' cycles! "When he came dashing in with seconds to spare on the timer, we all cheered, and everyone was glad to spend a few extra minutes folding clothes because of his ingenuity—and there we all were at 10:30 on a Saturday morning, free as birds for the rest of the day."

Wayne and I tried this approach one Saturday when we all decided it might be nice to spend the afternoon at Sturbridge Village, a delightful re-creation of a late 17th-century New England town in southern Massachusetts. The laundry had been done for the week and the beds changed, but the vacuuming and dusting and car washing all remained before we could, in clear conscience, depart. "Do whatever you think you can do well for the next thirty minutes," we told Rick and Jenna. "We'll all work as hard as we can until eleven o'clock, and then no matter what hasn't been done yet, we'll stop and go to Sturbridge." I flew through the house with the vacuum cleaner while Rick followed with the Pledge and a dustcloth, and Wayne and Jenna tackled both cars simultaneously—he on the outside with bucket and hose and she on the inside with the Windex and car-vac. When the timer rang at eleven o'clock, we reassembled in the kitchen, flushed but triumphant, to pack a picnic lunch for our outing. Wayne and I accomplished probably three-quarters of the actual work, but everyone had given his best for an equal amount of time.

The concept of equal sharing of household tasks is one important element in a nonsexist upbringing, but the way those tasks are divided among boys and girls is equally critical. In more and more households, the domestic double standard is being undermined successfully by parents who consciously chip away at traditional ideas about house maintenance, such as that women cook and clean while men repair and mow. Because our children will eventually adopt more of our values than either we or they believe they will at this moment, it is essential that we do everything in our power to present satisfactory role models. By making sure that my daughter sees Mom right out there with Dad raking the leaves every autumn, I do not expect to create a great enthusiasm in her for leaf-raking. I have no such enthusiasm myself, but then, neither does her father. The fact is, the leaves must be raked, and there is no biological or moral determinant involved in deciding who can rake them. And when Wayne swears his way through sewing on a shirt button in full view of his son, he is not communicating to Rick a fondness for needlework. He is merely demonstrating that it is useful to know how to sew on one's buttons, since they detach themselves from men's shirts as well as women's blouses with equally irritating frequency.

Our children are too much of an age for babysitting ever to become an issue. By the time Rick is old enough to be left alone, his sister will be too. In families where the age-spread among the children is greater, though, a wonderful opportunity exists to expose both boys and girls to the responsibilities and rewards of child nurturing. Remember Cassie MacNamara, the executive secretary and mother of nine, including two sets of twins. Her approach to the care of the youngest of her brood is as nonsexist as it is practical, with each older child of either sex responsible for the daily supervision, on a rotating basis, of one younger child. (Her oldest son, now in college, is out of the line-up.) Whether the task be helping with clothes or bath, packing a lunch for school or reading a bedtime story, each little one is quite accustomed to having it done or supervised by an older sibling of either sex—as accustomed, in fact, as the older kids are to doing it. I like to think that there are nine more people in the world whose future husbands, wives, and children will benefit from this marvelous family interaction.

Though my children will not have this experience, I hope they will both choose to babysit for others' kids in future years, but I suppose that will depend to a great extent on the attitude of their peers toward their doing so. I know of one or two boys who babysit, my teenage nephew among them, but that doesn't exactly constitute a trend. Perhaps TV shows like, "Who's the Boss?", "Charles in Charge," and "Mr. Belvedere," which feature men of varying ages as housekeepers and child supervisors, will serve a useful purpose here. We'll have to wait and see.

Despite the reluctance of older generations to support nonsexist roles within the family, there is overwhelming evidence of progress being demonstrated by our children. My neighbor Tina commented on this recently while talking about her daughter Jessica and son John. "When an older person says something to Jessica like, 'Girls don't do that kind of thing, Jessica,' I don't think she gives a good hoot. Maybe some of it takes, but I know that Jessica is already considering the options of having children and whether she should go to work. 'Do you think I should have children, or do you think I should work first?' she'll say to me. It probably comes from listening to me because I'm always saying to her, 'What should I do, Jessica?' But yeah, she thinks about it. John also thinks about having kids someday. It's interesting."

In terms of household tasks, Tina's children are beginning to pitch in, "but I find that John says stuff like, 'I'll shovel the driveway and mow the lawn,' and Jessica likes to do the laundry. I'm sure they pick this up because they see me and Bill doing those things, but it does irk me. I would like to see them have nonsexist jobs in the house, but I don't know if that will ever come about." Occasionally, she says, the children surprise her by volunteering for a task traditionally performed by the opposite sex. "Bill can't cook at all, but every now and then, he'll try to make something. He was making eggs one morning, apparently not very successfully, and John jumped up and said, 'Oh, I'll do it!' And he did, very well."

My niece Patti's children are still very small (five, three, and three months), but she is already considering how she can instill nonsexist attitudes. "In Scott's room, there may be trucks and what have you, but he plays in Leah's and Amanda's room just as much, where they have dolls and a kitchen set and so on. At this age, of course, what I expect of them is the same, like putting away their clothes and their toys; but just because Scotty's the boy, I'm not going to make him mow the lawn. He'll be doing the dishes, and Leah will be using the lawn mower, too. The same with washing cars and so forth. A lot of that has to do with the way I was brought up. I have a sister and two brothers, and the dishwashing and the housework was always divided up equally—which isn't to say it really always was, but it was supposed to be."

In her daughters, especially, Patti is striving to foster a sense of unrestricted opportunity. "Of course, Leah's only five, so she wants to do everything she sees. We had a belly dancer for a friend of ours a couple of years back, and she wanted to be a belly dancer. She saw something about astronauts on TV, and she wanted to be an astronaut. But I want her to think as far ahead as she can, and I keep saying to her, 'You can be anything you want to be.' She was staying at my sister-in-law's house one weekend, and she said she wanted to be a father when she grew up. My sister-in-law told her that wasn't possible, but Leah insisted. 'My mommy told me I can be anything I want to be!' And if Scotty wants to be a nurse when he grows up, that's okay, too."

As children mature, their liberated upbringing ideally will broaden to include exposure to the equal financial relationship of the family wage-earners. Our children are reminded regularly that both Wayne and I share the responsibility of supporting the family, and we make it a point to discuss major purchases in front of them, weighing the trade-offs that these inevitably involve. For example, the newest of our two cars is five years old, and expensive repairs are beginning to crop up, prompting us to think longingly about trading it in on a new model. Even with a trade-in, though, a new car will mean years of substantial monthly payments, and we are trying hard to save enough to add another room to the house to serve as my office. Since we both earn reasonably good incomes, Rick finds it hard to understand why we can't do both, so we drag out the monthly budget book and explain the situation as simply as we can. "This is how much money we expect to earn in April, and here are the expenses we know that money will cover. That's if nothing unexpected comes up, and something unexpected always comes up." Like what, he wants to know. "Like the washing machine dying, as it did last month. The new one cost more than $400. Like your father catching pneumonia and your sister contracting the world's worst case of poison ivy and me losing a filling all in the same week, which cost plenty in doctors' bills and prescriptions. Like the emergency trip to the vet when Georgie got bitten by the neighbor's cat. Like replacing my eyeglasses when you sat on them in the car." Okay, okay, he gets the drift. "So, allowing a couple of hundred dollars for things like that, this is what we have left of the money we will earn to put toward a car payment or to put in the bank toward the new room. It's not enough for both, so we have to choose which one we want more."

That sinks in slowly. Apparently, it has never occurred to him that even grownups are restricted. "Who gets to decide?" is his next question, and I explain that Daddy and I decide together because we share the responsibility of spending our combined incomes in the best interests of everyone in the family. It seems like a good time to point out that he and Jenna will soon be involved in financial decisions affecting the family, as well. "Really?" he exclaims with delight, eyebrows scaling his forehead. Well, sure, I explain. "Remember last summer when we decided that we could go to Disney World in November if we cut out day-trips and so on during our summer vacation? We told you and Jenna that was the way it would have to be if you really wanted to go, and you agreed. So you were really involved in that decision. We had to choose, and you guys helped us decide. We'll be doing more of that kind of talking as you get a little older, like discussing how to pay for your college educations and your car insurance and things like that. When you're sixteen, you might even want to take a part-time job to help pay for those things, depending on your schoolwork load. You can work during the summers, too."

Instead of dismaying him, this news strikes him as good, and he decides on the spot that he will drive a truck. In future weeks, I find him watching carefully as I make out the checks. He is shocked at the sum I am signing over to the bank in the form of a mortgage payment, which I assure him is half of what some of our friends who bought houses more recently than we must pay. "Wow," he comments thoughtfully, and I agree. Better get used to it now, Kiddo, I think. After a deep silence, he cheerfully announces his intention to marry a rich lady and bounces back into the family room to watch cartoons. So much for the financial facts of life.

My friend Marie recalled a similar session with her sixteen-year-old daughter, who seemed sadly unacquainted with economic reality. While doing a bi-weekly grocery shopping at the supermarket together, Marie continually had to ask Susan to refrain from tossing expensive and unnecessary goodies into the cart. "But why, Mom?" Susan complained, reluctantly returning a fancy frozen dessert to the bin.

"Because there's exactly one hundred thirty-one dollars left in the checking account, and we'll be lucky to get out of here for that as it is. Think orange juice, not cheesecake."

"But there's plenty of money in the savings account. You can just transfer some into the checking account by phone, can't you?"

"I can, but I won't," Marie replied firmly. "We budgeted so much for groceries this month, and that's what we're going to spend, no more. If I overspent the budget every time someone had a yen for cheesecake, there wouldn't be anything in the savings account, and unless you intend to support me in my old age, you'd better help me see to it that our savings continue to grow." Susan looked at her aghast. Support her parents? It was a disturbing new possibility.

Though she was glad to have had the opportunity to acquaint her daughter with some economic facts, Marie reported that Susan developed an irritating preoccupation with the status of the family finances after that. "I created a monster!" she told me later. "I brought home a new pair of running shoes for myself today, and the kid actually had the nerve to ask me if we could really afford them! I told her I didn't think my purchase had undermined her chance to go to college, but I'd watch it in the future."

Even when both partners have established themselves in lucrative careers and careful budgeting is no longer as necessary, parents are concerned about teaching their children the value of money—that is, he who wants must earn in order to get. In the first months following my acceptance of a high-paying new assignment, I was strongly tempted to indulge Rick and Jenna with new furniture for their rooms, new bikes and skates, snazzy new clothes—but I stopped in the nick of time when I remembered The Voltron Incident.

"The Voltron Power Force" is an action adventure cartoon show featuring a bunch of robots who fit themselves together to form Voltron, the defender of the universe, and the program is Rick's latest obsession. Apparently, he is not the only child in the country so afflicted, since savvy toymakers have invested millions in creating complicated and expensive three-dimensional replicas of Voltron and its components, which are heavily advertised on television. Naturally, Rick just had to have one, and his choice cost about twenty dollars. Since neither Christmas nor his birthday was coming up, we told him he had to save up for it, and we would help by paying him a quarter for odd jobs such as cleaning out the cars and dusting the bookshelves. He earned a little money this way, and when he combined his earnings with the contents of his piggy bank and came up with nearly the full twenty dollars, we got tired of hearing about it and made up the difference so he could make his purchase. Had he worked harder for it, he probably would have valued it more; but as it happened, he became bored enough with the toy in just a few days to allow his sister to take it to school, where she promptly dropped it and broke the head and an arm off. They arrived home from school—Rick outraged, Jenna tearful—and presented me with an emotional situation with which I was in no mood to cope at that moment, so again, I took the easy way out. I went out and bought Rick a new Voltron and glued the old one back together for Jenna. As you've probably guessed, I haven't seen either one since, except when I clean out the toy chest in which they both languish. So easily had they been acquired, the toys became valueless; and I had set an unfortunate precedent. And so, when my first big fee appeared in the mailbox, and my thoughts turned longingly toward white canopy beds and new desks, I took myself firmly in hand and the check firmly to the bank.

Just last night we all had an interesting object lesson in respect for one's possessions, as well as for the labor involved in earning them, but this time, Wayne and I were on the receiving end of most of it. While shampooing Jenna's hair, I suggested that after school today she and Rick and I run over to Sears to get new school shoes, and I was astonished when she burst into tears. Through half an hour of sobs and hiccups, she told me the sad little story of a shopping trip with Wayne about a month ago at Sears, during which she had managed to misplace her beloved Cabbage Patch doll Cindy, who had accompanied Jenna everywhere for nearly a year. Though she realized she had left the doll in the store the minute she and Wayne returned to the car, she said nothing, since for the better part of the last week we had both been on her case about her carelessness with things. And for nearly a month, she had remained silent and heartbroken, not knowing if she would ever see her Cindy again.

I was horrified. Had we been so intimidating that the child thought we valued "things" more than we did our daughter's feelings? After a month, it was foolish to think the doll would still be in the store's lost and found department, if indeed it had ever been turned in, and there was no way a new doll could make up for the loss of her precious baby. I rushed to consult Wayne, and though it was after 8:00 P.M., he called the store immediately to inquire. Somewhere, there is an angel who understands the hearts of little girls. Not only was the lost and found department open at that hour of the evening, but the gentleman who answered the phone was as tickled as he could be to report that Cindy, turned in by a kindly customer, had been occupying the place of honor in the department's glass window for the last month. Wayne took Jenna to collect Cindy on the spot, and I cannot express the relief we experienced, tempered by the knowledge of the month of anguish we had caused our daughter, however inadvertently. Then came a laugh—on Wayne.

To honor the occasion and to offer our thanks to the kind folks at Sears who had made it possible for Cindy and Jenna to be reunited, Wayne proposed that we take some pictures to send them with a thank-you note, and he asked Jenna to get the camera from the kitchen. She started to go, then turned back to her father with an evil grin on her little mug. "Sorry, Daddy, I can't get it. You left the camera at Grandma's last Sunday, remember?" In fifteen years of marriage, I can't ever recall having seen my husband blush, but I saw him do it last night.

There are many twists to the task of instilling a respect for possessions, as well as for the work that is the necessary prerequisite to acquiring them, but the trick seems to be treading a fine line between giving our children enough to enhance their lives and showering them with so much largesse that we overindulge them. For most parents in our circle, the master plan involves helping children to earn special items instead of giving them everything outright. Rosemary and Al, who are comfortable financially, are already formulating a policy in connection with their year-old son Ryan. "I've seen too many of my friends' children who have just been given things, like cars when they're in high school," says Rosemary, "and I really want Ryan to work for things. We're preparing now so we'll have money for his college, but there's a balance between how much you give the kid financially and how much he's expected to work. As long as I feel he's always working toward a goal, we'll help out. I don't want him to feel that all he has to do is sit back and we'll do it for him. I want it to be teamwork. I always said Al and I were a team of two, and I like to think we're a team of three now. We're all three going to work together to get what we want—some enjoyment, some free time, and some hard work, too."

Thus, though Ryan is still a baby, our friends have already thought this one through. Because they have decided to limit their family to one child and they make enough money to assure their financial security throughout a planned and active "retirement," they are aware of the need to avoid handing Ryan everything on the silver platter they have earned.

For couples lacking substantial financial resources, the problem becomes one of making choices, and it is interesting to note how many parents are now involving their children in such family decisions, much as Wayne and I plan to do. By including our children in the give-and-take of every aspect of family life, be it housework, child care, or the earning and disbursement of family funds, we can spare them much of the floundering so many of us have had to do to achieve an appropriate balance of responsibility in these areas and go a long way toward laying the domestic double standard to rest in future generations.

3

COPING STRATEGIES

As our struggle for equality continues, it's clear that we have much to gain by doing everything in our power to eliminate the domestic double standard in future generations. It would be unrealistic and counterproductive, however, to refuse to acknowledge its existence in our present lives.

And so, while we do what we can to hasten its demise, we must also find ways in which to make the DDS more tolerable for the moment. Here, the experiences of our contemporaries can be helpful. In this section, you'll become acquainted with dozens of working wives and mothers who, though eager to banish the DDS, have learned to cope with it in the meantime. Their practical suggestions will help you manage maternal responsibilities more comfortably, evaluate employment options, deal with a number of life's little nuisances more effectively, examine new approaches to holidays and other traditional events within the extended family, and manage your time more efficiently.

Having a child means incredible fatigue, an enormous amount of extra work, little or no time for yourself, and a drain on your income. It also means a joy that defies description—and that makes it all worthwhile.

WHAT NO ONE EVER TELLS YOU IN LAMAZE CLASS

IN 1975, LIKE MOST ECSTATIC parents-to-be of that era, Wayne and I enrolled in Lamaze class and prepared ourselves diligently for our baby's birth. For some reason, the birth was always the main thing. My reading, nutrition, work schedule, and doctor's visits were all concerned with the safe delivery of the infant within me. Perhaps it was a last gasp of denial of the new responsibilities that awaited us. Perhaps it was a superstitious attempt to avert heartbreak should the child not be born healthy. Whatever, we focused on the impending birth instead of impending parenthood—with comical results.

Though a bit small at six and a half pounds, Ricky showed every sign of good health and wailed lustily seconds after his delivery. I remember smiling at that sound as I lay there. It would be the last time I did so. There has probably never been a woman as ill-prepared for the realities of motherhood as I was.

At some bizarre hour of the night, a nurse appeared at the door of my room bearing a screaming bundle. "Feeding time!" she announced cheerfully as I struggled up on one elbow. "You're kidding!" was my astonished response. "It's the middle of the night!" But middle-of-the-night feedings were just the first of a number of unpleasant new facts of life with which I would have to deal, like colic, and milk intolerance, and dozens of dirty diapers in a single day, and isolation, and . . . but why go on? The point is, how had I escaped this practical knowledge in my twenty-nine years?

It was a question I had occasion to ponder often during the next several months, which constituted my on-the-job training program in motherhood—and in the domestic double standard. It is only recently, nine years and another baby later, that I have had an opportunity to compare experiences with other new mothers and to conclude that my shameful ignorance was not really all that uncommon for women of my age. Lulled by the image of beautiful new mamas and their even more beautiful infants that were presented to us in advertisements for baby food and disposable diapers, and our natural doubts that it could all be that easy allayed by the euphoric cluckings of older female relatives who had forgotten the bad parts of their own children's babyhoods, we painted our nurseries a bright, nonsexist yellow and lumbered off to the hospital, oblivious to the major life crisis which awaited us.

It wasn't so much the work involved, I reflected again and again as I washed and sterilized bottles, mixed formula, laundered and folded diapers and crib sheets and tiny undershirts, fed and burped and bathed and walked and entertained and dressed and changed my infant son. It wasn't even the fatigue, which was considerable and unavoidable, I decided in the middle of many a night as I paced the cold floors in a vain attempt to quiet the squalling, red-faced scrap of humanity in my arms. And the isolation of a new mother, who has been accustomed to years of daily adult interaction via her job, can be accepted as temporary. It was the realization that this new being had forever altered my hard-won status as an independent person, far more so than Wayne's. Somehow, they never got around to mentioning this in Lamaze class.

And so, as the months passed and Wayne handled one 2:00 A.M. feeding to my ten, I became a mother. As he whistled his way out the door to work every morning, leaving me to my unpaid maternal chores, I reflected rather grimly that no one would do this for money anyway, only for love. But I had no choice but to acknowledge the domestic double standard that motherhood almost inevitably imposes.

A few months later, half-crazed with the monotony of full-time motherhood, I returned to work. This added nine hours a day, five days a week, to my basic work load while gaining only enough income to offset the costs of full-time day-care, transportation and parking, wardrobe replenishment, and additional income tax, since my earnings put us into a higher bracket. Still, working had undeniably positive results. For forty-five hours each week, I regained my sense of autonomy and slid gratefully back into the Before Motherhood Me—almost. And as unrewarding financially as my job was, at that point I needed it. The daily contact with adults who did not define me as a wife or mother; the knowledge that I was earning money, regardless of how little I netted; the varied texture of the work day as opposed to the sameness of at-home days—all of these things shored up my sagging self-esteem, which is a common condition among new mothers.

My friend and neighbor Tina calls the syndrome "burnout," and I guess that's as good a word as any to describe it. "John came along in 1975, and I found having the baby was wonderful. There were times when I was very tired, but I really enjoyed just staying home and taking care of him . . . until he was about six months old, and then I think I had burnout. Actually, I have a theory about this, because it happened at six months with each of my three children. I stopped breast-feeding in that general vicinity, or cut down, and so the hormones were changing, plus that's when all my kids started teething. All of a sudden, they went from sleeping all night to not sleeping at night. At that time, with all three children, I thought I was just going to say, 'That's it. I'm leaving this house, and I never want to be a mother again.'

"With each child, though, it lasted a smaller amount of time, because I knew it was coming, and I knew what to do about it. With John, my first, I was kind of isolated. That's when I decided to go back to school, and I found that just going out twice a week on my own got me through it. With Jessica, my second child, I started playing racquetball. I think exercise is the very best thing for it, though it's also important to have your own time, to say 'This is what I'm going to do, and just leave me alone.' I still do that with my kids. On school vacations, when they don't want to go to the racquetball club, I'll say, 'Look, this is my time.' Sara, my youngest, has been going with me since she was three weeks old." Now that Sara is almost four, Tina has returned to work part-time, even though her doing so is not a financial necessity. "Having a job has several benefits," she maintains. "You have the economic benefit, a renewed sense of your own worth, and also, just getting away from it all. It helps to get yourself in order, knowing that you have to get these things done. And it's nice to know that you're bringing in a paycheck. It gives you that worth. When you've got little kids at home, and you feel boxed in, your self-worth goes down the drain."

My twenty-six-year-old niece Patti agrees with this assessment. Also the mother of three young children, ages five, three and three months, she has found returning to work a key to restoring the self-esteem that new mothers frequently lack. "My first idea was that I wanted to stay home when I had kids. Then Leah came along. Some days you think, 'Oh, this isn't so bad,' but those are the days when you have other people around. When you're alone with her all day long, you're constantly thinking, 'I wish I had some time for myself, that someone would come and take this kid away for awhile.'"

Patti's feeling of isolation intensified with the birth of her two other children, Scott and Amanda, leading her to explore a number of work-at-home options before seeking part-time work outside her home. She now works approximately fifteen hours a week typing case reports for police officers at the town's police headquarters, a job she can perform evenings when her husband can be with their children. "I need to get out and work," she says. "I want the responsibility of my kids, but I also want to be making money for my own self-respect, to be with other people. My day starts at dawn and doesn't end until I fall into bed at night after work, but it's worth it. It's more than worth it."

For Tina and Patti, part-time work serves many useful purposes, providing a much-needed break from the twenty-four-hour-a-day role of mother, keeping them in touch with other adults, restoring self-esteem that is often eroded by the unpaid nature of their maternal duties, and adding somewhat to their families' incomes. Most importantly, it also helps them to cope with the domestic double standard that mandates that they be their children's primary caretakers.

Even when a couple's financial resources permit the hiring of household help to give a new mother some personal freedom, the domestic double standard is present. Having a child was a goal that Rosemary and her husband Al, for example, postponed until they were well along toward reaching their goal of financial independence. It was eleven years after their 1970 marriage that they focused on becoming parents. "We wanted a lot of freedom," Rosemary explains, "a lot of choices and options in life. We thought, if we plan ahead and work hard, maybe it will work out. So after we had made good progress financially and had both gotten established in our careers, we turned our attention to having a baby."

Rosemary was thirty at that time, and she and Al soon discovered that the best planning in the world cuts no ice with Mother Nature. "Just because you plan it doesn't mean it's going to happen. We had planned that I would have a baby by the time I was thirty-three, but I had infertility problems. When we had pretty much given up and decided we would adopt, I finally got pregnant."

Rosemary actually had her baby when she was thirty-six. Despite the admonitions of friends like me who tried to tell her that the baby was going to have more of an impact on her life than she thought and that he would consume more of her time and energy than anyone thinks possible pre-birth, Rosemary had, typically, planned an extremely full schedule of activities for herself during the year following his birth. She enrolled in a Ph.D. program, arranged to conduct management-training seminars at regular intervals for a client company, and planned lengthy visits to relatives scattered across the country, intending to take the baby with her. "Are you really sure you want to do all that?" we tried to caution her, wiggling our eyebrows madly at each other, but there was no deflecting her.

A long-term planner by nature, Rosemary had taken what she felt were sufficient steps to make her transition to motherhood a smooth one. During her pregnancy, she hired a high-school girl as a mother's helper and trained her to do everything around the house. Despite this very sensible approach, the reality of being a newborn infant's primary caretaker was something of a shock. "The biggest shock to me was what it did to me physically, because I thought I had a very high energy-level. I was thirty-six years old, and I had a Caesarean. That was one thing. For another, no one prepares you for what it's like to be feeding a baby every two or three hours, which means that you don't sleep. People tell you that you'll be tired, but tired is such an understatement that it's not even the right word. My funniest story is the day I was so tired that I took the dog's heartworm pills instead of my vitamins!" Now Rosemary says she can understand how entertainers and politicians can be hospitalized for exhaustion, because she was right at that point herself. "Al would offer to get up and feed Ryan, but when the baby was awake, I was awake. It didn't seem to matter who actually fed him, so why should we both be exhausted? I'd be lying there wondering if Al was giving Ryan enough formula or worrying about how long it would take him to go back to sleep."

Still, Rosemary stubbornly refused to allow motherhood to restrict her activities, taking Ryan with her on a cross-country trip visiting relatives when he was just three months old. "After that trip, I came back and went to the doctor and said, 'Look, I've got mono. I wake up in the morning and feel like I can't make it.' And he said, 'No, you're just exhausted. You're trying to go too fast,' because he knew I was trying to start my consulting business and had started graduate school at that point. So, my advice to anyone having a first baby, even if you can afford to hire household help, is to try and relax as much as possible because you'll need all your strength to cope with not sleeping. Skip the entertaining. Try to have people visit you only for very short periods of time—and I don't mean an hour or two, I mean twenty minutes!"

When I asked Rosemary if she thought the first year of motherhood was very different from the first year of fatherhood, her answer was a resounding "Yes. The responsibility for everything to do with Ryan's well-being is definitely more mine than Al's. The planning and the organizing and the thinking ahead is all on the woman's shoulders." She is quick to add, though, that she believes the double standard imposed by motherhood can be changed, and she is taking steps to do just that in her family. "It's very difficult to tell Al, 'Look, you're not doing your fair share,' when he doesn't understand what that really means because he hasn't had to do it. So this spring, and again later on, I'm going to go with my mother or a friend on a three-day mini-vacation, and I'm not getting food or anything else prepared ahead of time. Al has agreed to this, because he knows I'm doing it for a couple of reasons. One, I want him to understand what it's really like to have this responsibility and maybe start to do a little more of the thinking ahead with me, and two, I think it's good for mothers to get away." In the meantime, she highly recommends the mother's-helper route to new mothers who can afford to hire one, an expense that a working mother, especially, will find justifiable during the first year of her baby's life.

Despite the rigors of the early months, most working mothers agree that having a baby was the most wonderful experience they've shared with their husbands. Having a child means incredible fatigue, an enormous amount of extra work, little or no time for yourself, and a drain on your income. It also means a joy that defies description—and that makes it all worthwhile. Rosemary agrees with this observation. "I've been surprised at how much I've enjoyed Ryan as a baby. Before this, I thought babies were kind of boring blobs, so I figured I'd put up with the baby part, because eventually, the child would be four years old and would be some fun. But my whole life was renewed by Ryan. I've got this child who's excited about the most mundane things. I show him a balloon, and his face lights up. He smiles and laughs about everything, and it's such a joy. I had heard that about a million times, but it really is a euphoric feeling to have a baby!"

Though every new mother's experience is different, they seem to agree that keeping your perspective is the main thing. You have to trust that eventually that wakeful infant will sleep through the night, outgrow his need for diapers, and let everyone in the family go on to bigger and better things. To a baby, every day is a fresh start, and there's always something to look forward to. It's an attitude his beleaguered mother will do well to adopt, too—especially when a new brother or sister makes an entrance.

As wonderful and as exhausting as the first-baby experience is, it cannot compare in every way with the experience of having a second, or even a third, child—events which require every bit as much thoughtful pre-planning. For despite popular opinion, two children are not just as easy to manage as one, and four cannot eat as cheaply as three. Then, too, it is the arrival of Child Number 2 that often underscores the domestic double standard, which first-time mothers only begin to acknowledge. We are every bit as tired, and even more deserving of assistance, since there is another child in the house who demands our attention as well as the baby, but because we are now "old hands" at motherhood, we are far less likely to get it. While it is true that being an experienced mother helps in many ways to cope with a second infant, it does not make you any less weary when you're getting up nights again; it does not make getting two small children ready to go somewhere any less like a Chinese fire drill; and it does not simplify scheduling problems that would challenge a Manhattan police dispatcher. There are new challenges in addition to the old. While you're going down the now familiar diaper/formula trail, you're also navigating the unfamiliar waters of sibling rivalry, toilet training, and nursery school on behalf of your older child. Not to put too fine a point on it, things can get very complicated with two children—and darn near impossible with three—when you're a working mother.

The two keys to survival for those who opt to have more than one child appear to be thoughtful spacing between those children—at least two years, and three, if possible—and top-quality day-care. Had we been even remotely aware that a second child was in our future, Wayne and I would have done better at spacing our children; but since we had been assured that my first pregnancy was nothing less than a miracle, we did nothing to plan (or prevent) a second. I can therefore tell you from personal experience that seventeen months is not enough space between babies. Two in diapers, two not sleeping through the night, and two to pack up for day-care every work day was not twice as difficult as one—it was at least four times as difficult, physically and emotionally. I also try not to think about our budget some ten years hence when both kids, who are just a year apart in school, are in college—but that's another story.

Though we didn't do well at spacing, we were always extremely fortunate in the quality of day-care that was available locally. When Jenna was just a few weeks of age, I turned her over with complete confidence to my good friend, and the kids' surrogate mother, Marsha. With two small children of her own, Marsha preferred to stay at home and care for my kids during the work week to make her financial ends meet, and I will always be grateful to her for being there for us. My children adored her and thought of her sons, Brian and Todd, as their brothers. Marsha's Brian and my Ricky were so close in age and so similar in appearance, in fact, that the local merchants thought they were twins when Marsha took the crew out shopping during the day. For two full years, the four kids played, ate, squabbled, napped, walked, visited the library, built forts and made mud pies, went through toilet training, and enjoyed Marsha's loving attention, and when her husband was transferred to New York at the end of that lovely period, I was certain my working life was over.

Again, though, I was fortunate in that my children were members of the "second baby boom" created by parents who, like me, were products of the first boom following World War II. The exploding infant population in our suburb created an extraordinary demand for good day-care, and several centers had popped up within five miles of our home. Thanks to Marsha and her wonderful family, my kids had learned very early to live comfortably in a group situation, so separation anxiety was not a big problem for us. After visiting three centers in the area, I selected the one farthest from us geographically but closest philosophically to what I was seeking: a cheerful, loving environment in which structured time and learning experiences were skillfully blended with free time and supervised play. Named for the owner's three children, Caresa-Jo Day Care operated in the lower floor and back yard of a comfortable raised ranch, and the women who staffed the center were exceptionally caring and well-qualified people.

Not every mother is as lucky, of course. It is a well-publicized fact that there is not enough good day-care to go around in this country, and what is available ranges from overpriced centers with degreed professionals to less-than-sanitary group homes in inner cities. According to a March 1985 NBC News "White Paper," about 15 percent of all day-care children are now in group centers, from nonprofit operations in church basements to national chains with branches all over the country—"the McDonald's of day-care." By far the largest group, about 40 percent, are still cared for, as mine were originally, by the traditional "lady down the street," and another 30 percent are cared for in their own homes by their fathers, who work different shifts than their mothers, or by a grandparent or other relative.

The best estimate, according to NBC News, is that more than ten million American children are now enrolled in day-care, and the number is rising, yet only a few employers are beginning to respond to this urgent need in the work place. And because most employers remain inflexible about encouraging the shared parenting of even very young children by allowing fathers more flexible work schedules, it is primarily mothers who must cope. To do so, women are thinking carefully before expanding their families, returning to work only part-time in many instances, and even abandoning jobs that are important to them personally and financially when good day-care is not available.

Planning plays a more important part than ever in their survival strategies, especially when there is more than one child in the family. Patti knows this to be true.

The toughest part of having three small children, she says, is trying to find enough individual time for each child. "With Amanda and Scott, who are home with me during the day, it's not that hard to do, but when Leah comes home from school at 3:30, I'm getting dinner ready and getting myself ready for work, because as soon as Tommy walks in the door, I have to leave. I'm telling you, I get down to planning that I'm going to be playing a game with the kids at a certain time or reading them a story!"

In addition to meticulous planning, Patti is soliciting her husband's help more actively than she did previously, especially when it comes to preparing three children and two adults for a family outing. "Whenever we went out as a family in the past, I found that Tommy was getting himself ready, while I was getting myself and all the kids ready. Now I've gotten to the point where I'll say, 'Do this.' I can't just say, 'Tommy, get the kids ready,' because he hasn't done it and doesn't know where to start. So now I've started asking him to do very specific things at times like that."

However many children one has, and however difficult the "day-care years" are to manage, a working mother should not make the mistake, as I did, of assuming that life will become simpler once her children enter school. During those early years of motherhood, when the work week was endlessly complicated by the need to arrive at Jenna's day-care center and Rick's after-kindergarten play group at rigidly fixed times, I cheered myself with a vision of that wonderful day on which both children would walk hand in hand to the end of our driveway and board the big yellow bus for a full day of school—the same school, during the same hours. On that magical morning, I felt certain, my life would fall gently into place. My surprise was equalled only by my dismay when I discovered that in the 1980s, schools' expectations of parents have escalated enormously—and to a teacher, "parent" still means "mother."

Despite the fact that the great majority of mothers are as fully employed as fathers, an annoying number of permission slips, notices, forms, invitations, and other school communications are addressed to "Mrs. Sprankle." It is only when I do some less-than-subtle reminding that our children's teachers remember Wayne's existence. He has never, for example, been asked to be a "Room Father." And it is always I who am requested to bake the cookies for the Christmas party, to accompany the class on a field trip, to sew the costumes for the recital or play, and to supervise a booth at the annual school picnic—and I who am made to feel a piker when I decline to do so. I find this especially surprising in light of the fact that most elementary school teachers are women, and presumably, working mothers themselves, but there it is. Perhaps it is merely a carry-over from the days when out-of-home employment was unusual among the mothers of school-age children; or perhaps, as I believe, we women are partly at fault for allowing this manifestation of the domestic double standard to go unchallenged. It's time we helped educate our children's teachers about the facts of the two-career family life, but in the meantime, we cope.

The mothers of kindergarteners are often shocked at the amount of paperwork that is involved in shepherding children through school. It is usually most burdensome during the first couple of weeks of each school year, when health officials clamor for lengthy verification of each child's health, eyesight, hearing, and a summary of his or her innoculation history; the PTA zealously recruits members and contributions; the town recreation department announces its fall program sign-ups; and every conceivable school regulation changes. When Ricky first entered school, emergency notification forms, bus routes and regulations, calendars, snow-day procedures, lunch menus and payment instructions, requests for smocks on art day and sneakers on gym days, name tags to be pinned between shoulder and waist for two weeks only, invitations to meetings, hearings, conferences, and family suppers—plus a terse announcement that no child would be permitted to wear shoes with black rubber soles, like the two pairs I had just purchased—burst from his knapsack each afternoon while I imagined myself in mortal combat with some crazed bureaucrat who cranked out endless purple dittos in an attempt to bury me.

But once the tide ebbs around the first of October, reducing the flow of paper to a more manageable pace, it's mostly a matter of keeping up with it on a daily basis. I find that if I sift through the day's offerings while the kids are at the supper table, it works out well, since they're handy to explain what the Super Store really sells and why I'm expected to purchase two D cells and six asphalt shingles by next Tuesday. I have also learned to scrutinize each fill-in-the-blanks type form carefully in advance to determine whether or not I really have to complete it. For example, anything that begins, "We are required by the State of Connecticut Health Authority to . . ." is a must, but a form headed, "We find it helpful if we know something about . . ." is my option. Permission slips get signed and returned to the knapsacks immediately, accompanied by the necessary check or, more onerous, exact change. It's worth it to keep a jelly jar full of dollar bills, quarters, and dimes handy, along with a supply of small envelopes in which to seal them safely.

Next comes a quick review of the day's schoolwork, with which I could fill a moving van by year's end, I'm sure. Everything is taught via workbook these days, supplemented by the ubiquitous dittos, and it's not at all unusual for each kid to complete and lug home a dozen sheets of paper a day. After a year or so of conscientiously reviewing every addition problem, every spelling word, and every penmanship exercise, as seemed to be expected of me, I rebelled. If Rick or Jenna has a major skill problem, I expect to be informed. Otherwise, daily school work hits the trash basket within minutes of arriving at the house.

Finally, we have the sales messages, and there are plenty of them in the course of a year. What with individual and class pictures, at least two book fairs, PTA-sponsored sales of school supplies and Christmas presents, school rings and sweatshirts, and the variety of learning aids so freely peddled via the children, a family's budget can effectively be destroyed unless strict rules are enforced. Jenna and Rick may each purchase the lowest-priced photo package (How many wallet-sized prints do we really need, after all?), one book per fair, and ten dollars worth of Christmas presents for the other members of the family at the PTA's Holiday Shop . . . and that's it, unless they choose to pay for a special item themselves from their allowances.

As irksome as the paperwork is, it is at least possible to choose a relatively convenient time to do it. The personal summonses are far harder to accommodate. My children's school mandates a minimum of two parent/teacher conferences per child per year, and attendance at the annual school open house is an implied command performance. (By the time they get through psyching up the kids, I'd be a monster not to appear.) If you add PTA meetings, school plays and concerts, picnics, fairs, fundraising events, and the like, you can easily wear yourself ragged weeknights from September through June unless you set limits and stick to them.

Among the personal appearances requested, the parent/teacher conferences are naturally a top priority; but despite the fact that most mothers now hold full-time jobs, the great majority of these are routinely scheduled during the normal school day, necessitating complicated arrangements for parents who must request the time off during the day from their jobs or skip lunch to dash frantically to the school, conduct a hurried conference, and dash back to work. For a couple of years, I actually did this. Perhaps it was a childhood carry-over, the reluctance to make waves with school authorities. There is something about a summons from the school that strikes fear into the boldest executive heart. But when Rick entered the second grade, things changed. My current attitude is that my time is just as valuable as my children's teachers' time, and a certain amount of compromise is therefore in order.

Traditionally, I would receive a notice stating something like, "I have scheduled our fall conference for 2:45 P.M. on Thursday, November 11th," and I would meekly obey, regardless of the hoops through which I had to jump to appear at the appointed hour. This year, I informed both kids' teachers right up front—politely and in writing—that neither Wayne nor I could attend conferences in the middle of a working day, but we would make ourselves available as early as 7:30 A.M. or after 4:00 P.M. The next communication was addressed to "Mr. and Mrs. Sprankle," and it indicated that a conference would be possible at 8:30 A.M. on any of three suggested dates. Feeling that if the teacher was willing to compromise to the extent of coming in a little early, I could be no less gracious, I agreed to an 8:30 appointment and got to work just a little late. It wasn't perfect, but it was a start.

As a side benefit, I learned that early morning appointments with teachers have several advantages. First, you are both fresh, unfrazzled by the day's events yet to come. Second, such conferences tend to begin and end on time, since school begins promptly at 9:00 A.M. Afternoon conferences are always mushy, leaving you cooling your heels in the corridor while another child's parent drones on unrestrained after you've sped halfway across the state to get there on time. Third, your child, who is understandably anxious about what transpires during a conference, is spared an entire day with it hanging over his head. By the time the kid gets to school, it's all over. Finally, an employer is generally more willing to accept your appearance at work a bit late than he is your leaving early, since most crunches on the job occur at the end of the day. Besides, since you generally live closer to the school than you do to your place of employment, attending a conference on the way into work is far more efficient than running back and forth from your job in the middle of the day.

Dolores, the mother of three sons aged eighteen, fifteen, and twelve, has found the direct approach to teachers on this issue very effective. "I think they like the parent involvement, and they want to take that extra step to help. If you say you can come in only at 7:30 in the morning, then the teachers try to accommodate you, so if Kip and I both want to come in at that time, we can. In our family, Kip starts work later in the morning than I do, so he'll usually go to a conference before school. If I'm going to go to the conference, I'll schedule it for the last appointment of the afternoon and leave work a little bit early. We switch, too. If Kip sees Kenny's teacher during the first conference period of the year, then the next time, he sees Brad's teacher, and so on."

Now that their sons are in middle and high school, Dolores points out another problem. "They don't spend the day in a single classroom with one teacher like they do in elementary school. You've got to go from teacher to teacher. So on open-house night, we sit down and look at their schedules and decide who we're going to see. We could each take one child's schedule, as I've seen other parents do, but I like to do it together."

Dolores finds the teachers in her town's school system very attuned to the needs of working parents. "If there's a problem, they'll call you at night to discuss it. I think they're recognizing the fact that most parents work now, especially when you get up into the upper grades, because that's when most people really need to supplement their incomes for college that's coming up."

Extracurricular activities are another time-consuming aspect of children's school-age years, and Dolores is well acquainted with the scramble involved in accommodating her boys' interest in sports, especially. "Sports have always been a big part of our lives, and that's a real commitment. All three boys play hockey, and there's always one who draws the 5:00 A.M. Sunday practice. As far as I'm concerned, they can skip it—I've always felt they'll love me just as much whether they play 5:00 A.M. hockey or not! But Kip feels that there is a commitment involved in being on a team, and you must be responsible. It's part of the boys' character-building and part of the reason for their being in sports, so if the practice is at five, he feels you go at five. So Kip has assumed the responsibility for driving them there. But I won't get up!"

Aside from the rigors of hockey season, Dolores and Kip juggle a year-round schedule of team practices and games around the demands of their jobs. "Kenny plays soccer and hockey; Brad plays soccer, hockey, and track; and Jeff plays hockey and baseball, so coping with each child's schedule gets very complicated. What we've done is find other parents that can take our sons to practices that start late in the afternoon, and we do the taking home at 6:30 or whenever. Other parents are very understanding of this as long as you fulfill your share of the responsibility. If you can't do it on one day, you do it on another weekday or on Saturday. You work it out. There is a lot of chauffeuring involved, but all of the mothers are going through this, so everyone is always very willing to carpool, which is wonderful!"

The school-age years present yet another logistical difficulty for today's working mothers. A typical school day lasts just six hours, while a typical work day lasts eight. Add another hour each day for the home-office-home commute, and it's not hard to identify a three-hour gap between children's in-school time and Mom's at-work time that can be difficult to bridge.

Johnene, an executive consultant and the mother of two, addressed this problem head on. "How do you juggle a daughter who's in gymnastics six nights a week, a son who's on the swim team and in the art club, and two parents who work long days and travel frequently? So I decided, all right. Let's use the old networking system and figure out who can do what. I identified my major need as being someone who could come in between 3:00 and 6:00 P.M., take care of the kids, and drive them wherever they needed to go. And I found a person! I couldn't believe it, but this person really existed, and it worked. Also, when my husband was out of town and I needed to go out of town, we had the same individual on call."

The after-school day care programs that are springing up throughout the country offer another excellent way to bridge the gap between school hours and quitting time for Mom. An outstanding program, called Newington Elementary Children's Care, Inc. (NECCI), has operated for several years in three of our town's elementary schools, and we were lucky enough to live in a NECCI school district. If we hadn't, I would have moved! Without Connie, Rhoda, Ellen, Molly, and all the other wonderful women who have staffed NECCI over the years, my life as a working mother would have been infinitely more stressful than it has been.

From 7:00 A.M. to 5:30 P.M. each school day, NECCI staff welcome and supervise the school-age children of working parents right on the school premises. Kids in kindergarten through grade five can attend any of the hours they are not in school. The fees are very reasonable, and there is a financial break given when more than one child in a family attend. With the NECCI program at my disposal, though at one point I had a daughter in kindergarten half days and a son in first grade from nine to three, I had no mid-day transportation with which to contend. Whenever school was over for each child, he or she just strolled down the hall to the NECCI room, got a healthful snack, and launched into play with children who were already friends from school. If Wayne was out of town and I had to be at work at 8:00 A.M., no problem. I just drove the kids to school early and let them play in the NECCI room for an hour before school, which they loved to do.

Better yet, NECCI operates during most school vacations—and all summer long. Both of my children have spent several contented summers playing, taking swimming lessons, participating in the town library's summer reading program, and attending children's plays and movies throughout central Connecticut, all under the supervision of NECCI staff. It's as close to being the perfect solution for working parents as anything I've come across: The children's NECCI playmates are also their schoolmates, so their adjustment to the group is quickly accomplished. There's no worry about after-school transportation, especially in bad weather, since the transition from school requires only a short walk indoors. The schoolyard is an ideal outdoor playground as well, since it is fenced in, well away from the street, and outfitted with a goodly variety of sturdy, child-sized play equipment.

If a town councilor or other elected official wants to assure political popularity, he or she should consider launching a program like NECCI. It's a sure-fire strategy to win the hearts and votes of every working mother in the district!

The demands of the domestic double standard on the working mother can be endless unless she takes charge of the situation, communicates what is possible and what is simply not possible to those who would demand too much of her, and creates a support network that includes anyone who can be helpful in the day-to-day juggling of schedules and activities. Accommodating the day-care, school, and extracurricular activities that frame her children's lives is a task that goes on for at least 18 years; but by thinking beyond the infant and toddler stages when mapping out a survival strategy, today's working mothers are doing a splendid job of working it out.

By accepting the givens of our lives, assessing our marketable skills, and fabricating new "jobs" that meet our individual needs, we are, along with thousands of other modern pioneer women, creating a new kind of employment market for those who follow.

HIRING AN EMPLOYER

"PAY EQUITY IS UNFAIR TO Women," ran the rather startling headline of a March 1985 FORTUNE commentary by Linda Chavez, staff director of the U.S. Commission on Civil Rights. She went on to state that while comparable worth sounds great for women in principle, it actually would have the effect of reducing job opportunities for women in the very employment categories to which they continue to gravitate for reasons quite apart from salary. "Earnings clearly play only a partial role in women's decision to work in a limited number of jobs. Of far greater importance is the need that most women have to balance the demands of a job with the responsibilities of family life."

By continuing to opt for sales, clerical, and other traditional female jobs, Chavez maintains, working mothers are making conscious, rational choices based on their desire for jobs that don't penalize them for temporary absences for childbearing, that offer regular daily working hours and proximity to telephones in the event of child-related emergencies. But comparable worth advocates appear committed, she says, only to a quick fix for the symptom—unequal rates of pay—rather than an examination of, and long-range cure for, the underlying problem. "It is as if they cannot conceive that women are capable of acting in their self-interest. It suggests . . . that women need protection from the consequences of their choices."

Well, maybe. I'm well aware of the reasons why working mothers settle for being underpaid and of the trade-offs they accept as a part of their juggling act. I'm just not convinced that a fairer distribution of household responsibilities, as well as equal pay, wouldn't go a long way toward relieving the burden imposed on women by the domestic double standard.

"If comparable worth becomes the law of the land," Chavez concluded, "higher salaries almost certainly will mean fewer jobs in traditionally female occupations." Okay. But if women, who currently earn only 60–72 percent of what men earn, depending on whose statistics you go by, received equal pay, how many *more* paid jobs might they be able to create in the areas of day care and home maintenance, offsetting jobs lost in clerical and sales areas? And might not the ripple effect elevate salaries in those fields as well? Would we not all be better off with the resultant sharing of the domestic/outside employment burden?

I do, however, heartily support Chavez' statement that today's woman is capable of making rational decisions about her employment, selecting from the options available to her on the bases of her financial needs and personal circumstances. I would go further than that, though. Not only are we capable of choosing, but we are capable of creating new alternatives to traditional employment opportunities.

I am personally well acquainted with three working mothers who, like me, have matter-of-factly assessed their marketable skills and job interests, decided the circumstances under which they might use them to best advantage and balance the many demands on their time—and gone for it. Each is married, has at least one child, and has worked for many years. Because I and my friends aren't such an esoteric lot, I can only assume that Tina, Patti, Rosemary, and I are representative of the potential that can be realized with thoughtful foresight.

My employment history is a checkered one, though not, I believe, atypical for a woman of thirty-eight today. Earlier I described my dissatisfaction with secretarial work, which led me to acquire a B.S. in Business Administration during my child-bearing years as a credential necessary to "professional" employment. I lusted after a fast-track career in corporate or agency communications, intrigued by the fun and creativity of ad writing; and by mid-1980, I had landed the job of my dreams: sales promotion copywriter for a Hartford-based insurer. How I did this remains something of a mystery to me, since I had no particularly relevant experience to offer. As I recall, I was working as a technical writer in the company's education unit when the corporate relations department asked for assistance on a complicated recruitment brochure, and one thing led to another.

Because I was at the height of my Superwoman phase at that time, I was determined to make a success of my new job and to keep everything on the home front running smoothly as well. For nearly three years, I did just that, outperforming every other writer on the staff between 8:00 A.M. and 4:00 P.M., then rushing through the commuter traffic to Ricky's school and Jenna's day care center before returning home to cook dinner, supervise baths, and so on and so on. When especially demanding projects came along on the job, I made special arrangements for the children (which usually consisted of imposing once again on my wonderful mother-in-law) and rose to the challenge. For a while it all seemed worth it. In corporate terms, I was rewarded for my efforts initially, receiving top performance ratings and handsome salary increases. My bosses—all four of them, in ascending order from copy chief to executive vice president—repeatedly lauded my performance, and I reveled in their stroking. But after three years of witnessing the incredibly complicated and pointless department politicking that had such a negative impact on myself and my colleagues, I'd had enough, and in July 1983, I walked away from the big bucks to reconsider what I wanted to be when I grew up.

My anguish during the ensuing nine weeks of unemployment, which felt more like nine years, was considerable. The issues were complex, and the practical realities loomed large. I needed to work, to maintain my sense of self and to bring in some money, but I was no longer interested in climbing the corporate ladder, where the top salaries were. My children, who were finally both in school and enjoying an after-hours play group right on the school premises, were content for the time being, but they would soon be too old for such rigid arrangements. They would want to join the Brownies and Cub Scouts, take music and dance lessons after school, and invite their friends home to play, and I believed they should be able to do those things. Wayne was twelve years into a twenty-two-year commitment to his law-enforcement career, which required long hours and frequent travel. He did not wish, nor did I wish him, to make a change. He enjoyed his work; we enjoyed his salary; and we would all enjoy his handsome retirement benefits ten years hence. Because he could not adapt his schedule to help meet the children's needs, I realized I would have to do so.

While I continued to mull things over, I accepted a position with a nearby university as a writer of fundraising proposals. The pay was not nearly as high as my corporate salary had been, but the hours and location were convenient, and the work was reasonably satisfying, though repetitive. The best thing about the job was the people. Say what you want about ivy-covered professors, academics are far more open to nontraditional employment alternatives than are business types, who fear endlessly for their bottom lines. Though I could not quite yet put my finger on how I would do it, I recognized an opportunity to redefine my career in that university setting. Here, I thought, I can begin to work something out.

The first step, as it is on any new job, was to prove myself—to demonstrate that my ability warranted serious consideration of any proposal I might subsequently make regarding out-of-the-ordinary employment arrangements. For six months, I was the perfect employee, arriving early, completing complicated assignments with minimal supervision, and never, never requesting time off or other special treatment. As anticipated, this superior performance was soon taken for granted, and I was expected to do more, better, faster, than were other members of the staff. While irksome, for the moment, this was all part of the master plan.

Next, I began accepting free-lance writing assignments from two or three regionally recognized corporations, announcing each highly paid project loudly and with great glee to my university colleagues. This had the dual advantages of hedging my bet—providing a cornerstone for a free-lance business, should I care to pursue it—and of elevating my worth in the eyes of my university employers, who could not hope to meet the corporate fees I was collecting on the side.

By April of 1984, I was ready to take things one step further, and I approached my supervisor with a proposal for part-time contractual work, carefully constructed to the university's as well as to my advantage. Instead of working seven hours a day, five days a week as a full-time employee, I offered to work eight hours a day, four days a week on a contract basis for the same "salary." The university would thus lose only three hours a week of my services but would net a savings of nearly twenty percent of the cost of my full-time employment, since it would no longer contribute to my Social Security or to my group life insurance plan or to the state's unemployment compensation plan on my behalf, and it would no longer subsidize the four weeks of paid leave to which regular, full-time employees were entitled. For my part, I would lose about 5 percent of my net income, since I would have to pay a self-employment tax, but I would gain one clear day each week to pursue more lucrative free-lance assignments elsewhere.

Though initially surprised, my supervisor and the

university's employment director assessed their needs and our relative bargaining positions very realistically and concluded, as I had hoped they would, that my proposal was workable. With some difficulty, since they had never before engaged a long-term staff member on a contract basis, they drew up a legal document covering a six-month period, at my request, and we embarked upon what we all viewed as a trial run of the new arrangement. Their fear, understandably, was that they were setting a dangerous precedent, prompting every other staff member to seek such flexible arrangements and wreaking havoc with their already complicated staffing pattern. I understood the problems, but I felt strongly that the availability of more flexible employment opportunities would ultimately work to the institution's advantage, attracting capable free-lancers the tuition-driven university could not hope to lure away from higher-paying, profit-making organizations on a full-time basis.

I am delighted to report that the experiment was a great success. I stuck conscientiously to the terms of our agreement, and after several months, even the doubters within the organization had to admit that nothing had been lost, and much had been gained, all around. A generic version of my contract became the model for other agreements between the university and free-lance vendors, who viewed the somewhat low pay rate as an acceptable trade-off for professional and personal flexibility.

In the ensuing months, I left the university to concentrate on two other accounts and my book projects, which combined, offer me the income and flexibility I need plus the creative stimulation of a variety of writing assignments. I was now completely self-employed, working the hours that suited me in the comfort of my own home.

Though Wayne was all for taking a loan to construct a home-office addition to the house, I convinced him that it would be more prudent to convert the living room into my office until we could afford to pay cash for the new room, probably a year from now. Since we have a large family room off the kitchen, equipped with TV and fireplace, we tend to spend most of our time there anyway, so the living room conversion would pose no hardship.

Next came the final commitment to my new enterprise: withdrawing Rick and Jenna from their after-school day-care program. I knew that having done so, I could not easily turn back, since there was always a lengthy waiting list for admission to the popular program; but on Thanksgiving Day, I took the plunge and announced that on Monday, the kids should take the school bus home at 3:15. At ages nine and seven and a half, they were ready for more unstructured time, and I was glad that my struggle for alternative employment had allowed me to accommodate that need. From now on, employment is no longer a one-way street for me, with potential employers doing the hiring. Today, I'm hiring my employers, with whom I negotiate the terms of our affiliations to our mutual satisfaction.

There are disadvantages to working at home, certainly. It requires a lot of self-discipline, for one thing, to put on clothes and at least minimal makeup to work in my living room; but in street clothes and lipstick, I can slip into the role of working writer far more easily than I can unbrushed and in my bathrobe. Then, too, my working hours are extremely limited during the week. Technically, the kids leave the house for seven hours, five days a week, but in reality, they don't. Last week, for example, Jenna was home for two days with poison ivy. The first three days of this week, Rick was home with the flu. Both are in school today, but Friday is a school holiday, and a week from now, they will both be home for ten straight days during April vacation. During parent/teacher conference periods, school is shortened by two hours on each of three days—and so on and so on. Sometimes, it seems as if the house never empties, and I cannot concentrate with the kids and their friends under foot. I cope by making it a point to be at my typewriter when the kids walk out the door in the morning and to ignore dust, streaky windows, dirty laundry, and the dishwasher that needs to be unloaded until they return. Those things, I *can* attend to when the kids are around.

At first, I thought it would be difficult to schedule client meetings during my limited work hours, but when I thought about it, most meetings are conducted between 9:00 A.M. and 3:00 P.M. anyway. So far, it has not been a problem. The pluses far outweigh the minuses, in fact. Ten hours a week have been added to my life, since I no longer have to commute to an office. I love being able to turn on Jane Fonda's "Workout" when my back kinks up and spend ten minutes unkinking with vigorous aerobics in total privacy. I fill the gas tank about half as often as I used to, and it's much easier to stick to my lifelong diet now that I'm not being asked out to lunch every other day. Sometimes I feel a bit isolated, but mostly not, what with client meetings, interviews, and the kids arriving home at 3:30. Too, my focus on my work is much stronger without the inevitable distractions of office politics. In every office in which I ever worked, an extraordinary amount of time was consumed each day in endless rehashes of who said what to whom and how so-and-so reacted. Now, they can all cut each other's throats as far as I'm concerned—it's no skin off my nose!

It seems very right for me not to tie my professional identity to a single organization any longer. I am comfortable moving among a variety of clients, coming together with one organization, then another, to address specific needs. I enjoy getting up in the morning and not being able to predict exactly what the day will hold, though having sufficient control over my schedule to accommodate my family responsibilities. I have come to this arrangement largely because of the domestic double standard, it's true; but by addressing the facts of my life head on, I have carved a satisfying professional niche for myself as well. Chances are, I would have opted for the life of a free-lancer anyway, but that old double standard provided the impetus to get me here sooner.

* * *

Working at home is not every woman's solution to the need to balance multiple roles, however. Though it sounds appealing to many at first, they find the stimulation of working outside the home to be what they really want from a job, in addition to needed income. My niece Patti is a good example.

Raised by a mother who worked full time for as long as she can remember, Patti is committed to "being there" for her children—aged five, three, and three months—but also needs to contribute to the family income for her own self-esteem, she says. At twenty-six, she has already experimented with at-home employment, but has found it unsatisfactory. "I tried every at-home thing I could. For a while, I did babysitting here when my daughter Leah was very small, and it was a way of bringing in money, but it got to the point where my mind was numb because all I was thinking of was kids, diapers, bottles. Then I did typing for a lawyer at home. I sold Tupperware and Avon. I did all of that, but it just wasn't enough. It wasn't just financial. We needed a second income, but I needed work for me, too. I needed to be with other people, to get away from the kids. I needed to be me again.

"I knew that I didn't want to work full-time, mainly because my mother did it; and when I was a kid growing up, I did not like it that my mother wasn't around. I really wanted to be available for my kids, but I needed to get out and work, too, so I got to the point where I wanted to try and arrange both." After some thoughtful consideration of her options, Patti decided her most marketable skills were secretarial, since she had worked as a legal secretary before the birth of her first child. She preferred part-time work, but part-time pay wouldn't amount to much if she had to incorporate day-care expenses into the budget. In any event, she strongly preferred to be with her children during the day. The most logical solution, then, was part-time secretarial work in the evenings, when her husband would be available to care for the children—but where could she find such a job?

In West Hartford's police headquarters, as it turned

out, where Patti now types police case reports approximately 15 hours per week, spread over three evenings and the weekend. "Usually, my hours range between fifteen and twenty, although at times I work full time if I take over for the Chief's secretary when she's on vacation or out sick. The job is great for me, because it varies. I don't have to go in on any certain days. I can work six hours one night or three. On the weekend, I can work six hours on either Saturday or Sunday, or I can spread the same hours over two days. The one drawback is that now that I'm going in nights, there's really nobody for me to talk to except maybe a few of the police officers that walk by, or the custodians! But when I replace the Chief's secretary, I'm in with the full-time staff."

Despite the extraordinary demands of three small children, Patti has discovered a way to meet her particular employment needs, which include significant income, a flexible schedule, and the stimulation of being with other working adults from time to time. While her present position meets these immediate needs, she considers it a stepping stone for the future, too. "When my youngest daughter is three, I'll probably begin looking for full-time work, but I won't be going out for the money only. Now that I've got a foot in the door at the police station, I wouldn't mind working there, but I'm very particular about the position I would accept—either the Chief's secretary or secretary to the Assistant Chief. Also, in the back of my mind, I've always wanted to go to college, but toward what, I couldn't even say. I go back and forth between so many things. I'm still considering whether I want to continue being a secretary and go along this line or whether I want to see about something else."

Whatever she decides three years hence, Patti feels she will be in a much better position to make a good decision at the age of twenty-nine than she was when she graduated from high school. "I'll be looking for a job that best fits my lifestyle—in other words, my need to be available for my kids—because they do come first, no matter what. Women who have to work strictly for financial reasons might take any job they can get, but I'm planning on finding something that is going to be best for me, that offers some flexibility. As much as possible, I'll 'give my all' to the job, because it's important to me to do that; but when the kids are sick and I can't arrange for someone to take care of them, I have to be able to take that time." As committed as she is to her children's well-being, Patti is well aware that she cannot live her whole life around them. She will be scarcely 40 when her youngest enters high school, and she is determined to avoid the empty-nest syndrome by balancing the elements of her life long before then. "Some days, I can't wait until the kids are grown so I can have more time for me, but then I think, 'When they're grown, and they don't need me, what's going to happen to me? Am I going to be able to handle that all right?' By working part time now, I'm keeping in touch with other things, so after the kids are grown—or in any case, once they're in school—I can go on to the next stage more easily."

My neighbor Tina also found working at home unsatifactory, although initially it seemed to meet some of her employment needs. At thirty-three, she too is the mother of three children, though at ages ten, seven, and four, they are quite a bit older than Patti's. Tina had never planned to work when her kids were young unless it was an economic necessity. She completed a degree in secondary education while she was pregnant with her second child, but it soon became clear to her that teaching was no longer a career that interested her. "I had planned to go into teaching until I had kids, and then I'd had it with kids. I was with them all day long, and I said, 'There is no way I'm leaving this house to go from kids to kids.'"

Now that her children are older, she is again considering going into teaching, but it's only one of the work options she is investigating. "I have nothing specific in mind, but I do have lots of thoughts. I can't really decide what I want to do when I grow up! I don't want to have a full-time, traditional office job, because I hate working in offices. They drive me wild. I find a lot of office work repetitious, and you're in that same office every day, year in and year out, with two or maybe three weeks' vacation. I have no desire to do that.

"I don't feel that I have to bring *x* amount of dollars, which is very nice. Bill will say to me, 'You know, if I were you, I wouldn't work at all,' but that's not what I want, either. I can't imagine what I would do with my time if I were home all day. Right now, I'm negotiating with the makers of a line of knapsack toy animals to be their New England sales representative. Something like that I would love. You can work as hard as you want and make as much money as you want. You're getting out and meeting new people, but when there's a day when the kids are sick, hey, that's it. I definitely want that flexibility. It's very important to me to be able to put my kids first when they need me. I chose to have children, and they're my job, at this point, so I'd just as soon do the best job I can."

Though her personal priorities are clear, Tina admits to feeling societal pressure to work outside the home. "It's like the big pull, saying you're not a full person unless you're out in the work world." That pressure has become an unpleasant backlash of the women's movement experienced by many who feel their peers are sneering at them if they choose to put their careers on hold for a while to be with their young children, or if they have no career aspirations at all.

"I think I will get into the work market, but unless I find something I really love, I don't ever see myself working a nine-to-five job, ever, even when the kids are older. There are times when even teenagers need you around." Too, Tina and her husband Bill love to travel, preferring to be able to pick up and go when an opportunity presents itself without worrying about two work schedules to adjust. For the moment, then, part-time work is all she is willing to consider.

Several years ago, when Bill, a salesman, was having a difficult year, Tina found the family in an economic crunch in the middle of the heating season and decided to look for work. "I wanted a part-time job, obviously, but I had no idea where to look, so I just sort of thumbed through the paper and found a marketing research job, which I eventually accepted. I worked there for about two months, but that job didn't work out at all. I had also written a letter to another firm that was advertising for someone to work at home. One day, this guy called me and said he had my letter, and when could I start? It turned out to be work on automobile insurance investigations, calling people and finding out how they're using their cars. It was very handy, because I could work at home the hours I wanted to work between 9:30 A.M. and 7:00 P.M. I quit the marketing research job immediately."

In some ways, her new job worked out very well, since she didn't have to pay for day-care, transportation, or an office-type wardrobe; and if there were days she wanted to take off, she simply took them. In other ways, however, working at home had its drawbacks. "When I worked at home, it was like I was a non-worker. If you asked any of the kids' teachers, they'd say, 'John's mother is at home.' Bill didn't even consider me a worker. He'd say, 'God, this house is a dump, Tina. What's the matter with you?'—that kind of thing." When her employer's office manager quit, though, things took a different turn—a turn for the better in many aspects. Because she had proved to be an exceptionally productive and reliable employee, her boss offered her the newly vacant position of office manager, which she at first refused. "I said I didn't want to work full time, and I didn't want to work in the office. A couple of months later, they asked if I'd job-share with the owner's wife, do three days a week, but I decided I didn't want to do that either. Finally they said, 'We're really interested, and you can pick any two days you want!' so I accepted, and now I work two full days a week in the office. It's fifteen hours a week, and if I want to bring work home and do it here, I can. I never know what I'll be making from one week to the next, but I like those days off. The woman with whom I job-share is very flexible with me, too. When

I have to pick Sara up after nursery school and drop her at day care, that's fine."

Though she really enjoys going out to work now, Tina maintains that she would hate to do it every day, finding job-sharing an excellent alternative. It's a preference shared by many mothers of young children, who enjoy the stimulation of working outside the home but who are reluctant to work more than part time.

Not every woman has a choice, of course; but those who do not have to work full-time are finding a growing number of ways to combine full-time motherhood with part-time employment. Consulting work is one such opportunity.

Rosemary, you may recall, is my friend who had her first and only child at the age of thirty-six, only slightly behind schedule according to her and her husband Al's master plan: think ahead, work hard, become financially secure, and then have a baby. Following their 1970 wedding, Al spent two years in graduate school before embarking upon an actuarial career with a Hartford insurance company, while Rosemary worked as a special education teacher and completed her master's degree. Teaching had always been her career choice, but after giving the profession her best for many years, she was forced to rethink her career goals. "I was a special education teacher in the Hartford school system until 1980, six years, and I'd have to say that I was happy for only three of those years. In 1980, I quit and changed my whole career focus. I became very disenchanted because of the odds against you on achieving success with anything—the kids, the parents, the whole school system. Realizing that I couldn't save the world was difficult, but it was another part of growing up. So I decided I wasn't going to beat my head against the wall anymore. I was going to do something that was more for me than for everybody else."

By that time, Al was well on his way to an outstanding career as an insurance executive and was totally immersed in his work. At first, his ambition left Rosemary feeling a bit stranded, but once she accepted the demands of his career, she turned her attention to her own. "I had to go through this whole thing of saying, okay, now what does this mean to me? What impact does this have on me—a good impact or a negative impact? For a while, it was very negative, but in the long run, it turned out to be very positive."

A teacher by education, and a person who is supportive of others by nature, Rosemary struggled to find a way to combine her skills and her personal attributes in a new career. "I decided I wanted to go into a business of some sort, and while taking a university course, I happened to meet the person who headed the management training department of a major corporation. Another man from that company was also in the class. He had often hired former schoolteachers to do supervisory training and to teach seminars for company personnel. We talked at length, and he arranged an interview for me."

Rosemary was hired for the job, and she discovered that she thoroughly enjoyed it. She designed and taught management training programs, developing new skills and applying previously acquired ones, for the next couple of years. She then moved on to senior training positions at two other area firms. After five years, she reached another turning point. "I felt I had reached a plateau in my career. After you're in training for five years, you go into management, or you go into consulting, or you just keep doing the same thing over and over. I wasn't interested in going into management at that time, though I may later, so I looked at other people around me who were consulting and decided to start my own business. Now I have my own consulting firm. At the moment, I'm the only person in the firm, but it's my own business!"

Rosemary now designs training programs in human resource development on a contract basis, primarily for insurance companies and banks, working as much or as little as she chooses while she devotes most of her time and attention to her son Ryan, born last spring. Though comfortable financially, she prefers to continue to work, though on a limited basis. "Either/or isn't enough for me—either a family or a career. I always wanted both. I've had to make choices about which was my priority, where I'm going to spend the majority of my time during a given period, and right now, my priority is my son. I limit my work. I have turned down some assignments because I just don't want to spend that many days away from him. Right now, I'm probably working about half the hours of a full-time job. I could go out and market myself and look for more work, but I want to spend more of my time with Ryan.

I prefer now to spend about 60 percent of my time with my son, 30 percent on my career, and 10 percent on myself and my husband. Maybe a year or so from now I'll spend 40 percent on my work and 50 percent with Ryan, because he won't need so much of my attention when he's in a nursery-school program. I'm still thinking about working full time, but I have to see how the consulting business goes. This year, I'm fairly well set, and I'll have to see if word-of-mouth advertising continues to be enough. I like consulting a lot. It pays very well. Even though I'm working half the days I used to, I'm earning much more per day, and with the tax write-offs, I'm bringing in close to what I was when I worked full time."

To balance the demands of career and motherhood, Rosemary is considering all the alternatives available to her for the next few years. "What I want for the future is a career that does not require 200 working days a year of my life. So, there are really three options for me. One is to continue as I am as a consultant, and if I go on attracting enough clients, I'll probably do that. If I find that the marketing isn't going well, I have another choice: I can go to work for a larger consulting firm and work out a schedule that meets my needs. Another option is to get a doctorate and try to teach in a university, which would give me flexibility, too. In fact, I've already been accepted into a program. I'll pursue one of these three options for the next five years. After that, I'm not sure."

What is sure is that Rosemary, like Tina, Patti, and me,

is aware that there are choices available to her and is making every effort to explore her options thoroughly. In the process, we are helping to create better options for the working mothers of tomorrow, who will benefit from the precedents we set. By accepting the givens in our lives, assessing our marketable skills, and fabricating new "jobs" for ourselves that simultaneously meet our individual needs and those of the people who hire us, we are creating, along with thousands of other modern women, a new kind of employment market for those who follow.

By refusing to settle for underpaid clerical, sales, and other low-paying part-time jobs over the long term, though we may use these as stepping stones to more lucrative and satisfying work, we are thumbing our noses at a national employment system that continues to ignore the needs of millions of working mothers and are taking charge of our working lives in creative new ways. Not only do we *not* need protection from the consequences of our choices, but where insufficient choices exist, we'll make new ones, adapting to the domestic double standard until we can lay it to rest.

Until we value ourselves and our roles as women as much as we value the roles of men in our society, we cannot expect men to reciprocate. This lack of self-worth is an unattractive and unproductive posture that reinforces the domestic double standard every day.

DEALING WITH LIFE'S LITTLE NUISANCES

THERE ARE A LOT OF little nuisances in the life of a working mother—some avoidable, some not. Dealing with them, or choosing not to, is all part of her strategy to cope with the domestic double standard, and each decision must be made on the basis of how important a positive outcome is to her and how much time and energy she can afford, on balance, to achieving it.

Repair people and delivery personnel who refuse to make specific appointments, doctors and dentists who keep their patients cooling their heels in waiting rooms as standard operating procedure, unpunctual people in general, mechanics who don't fix the car on the first visit, and babysitters who cancel at the last minute head my personal list of life's little nuisances. There are others, to be sure, but these inconsiderate folks are the ones with whom I have made a conscious decision to do battle in the hope that setting them straight will do much to eliminate the domestic double standard. In each of these cases, the underlying problem is the fact that the provider of the service considers his time more valuable than mine.

* * *

Case in Point: A small company in northwestern Connecticut offered to rent IBM personal computers for a day, a week, or a month and to eliminate the usual tangle of red tape that accompanies such a transaction. Since I needed one on a short-term basis, I drove out and rented a PC for a month; but I completed the assignment in question after only two weeks. I called the company to see what kind of a refund I'd get if I brought the equipment back that day, and the man who answered the phone at 9:10 A.M. told me I'd get a 20 percent discount.

Packing the equipment up carefully, I got three cartons and two kids, who were on a school holiday, into the car and drove the twenty-two miles back to the rental company, arriving at 12:30 P.M. The door of the office was locked, and there was no sign or note posted to indicate whether the occupants were gone for the day, out to lunch, or out of business. A waitress at a nearby restaurant offered the use of a telephone, but my call went unanswered. I was fit to be tied. There I was in the middle of nowhere with a carload of electronic equipment and two hungry kids waiting for lunch, and it looked as though I had made the trip for nothing. The man who had spoken with me on the telephone that morning couldn't have been the janitor—what had he been doing there, if not business, and why had he not done me the simple courtesy of mentioning the office would be closed that day? Because I was a woman calling from her home, I concluded, and promptly selected one more battle to fight.

I left a note stating that I had made a good-faith effort to return the PC and now expected a company staff member to retrieve it from my home and to deliver the 20 percent adjustment on my rental fee to which I was entitled. On Monday morning, I followed up by phone, and a sales representative reluctantly agreed to my request. I had a case, and he knew it, so reason, not anger, won the day. By refusing to accept his assessment of the value of my time, I succeeded in getting him to accept mine.

* * *

Case in Point: Our cat was due for her annual feline-enteritis booster shot. I called a local veterinarian who offered appointments, versus the come-in-and-wait-your-turn approach favored by a competing establishment, and scheduled a 9:00 A.M. visit in line with my belief that being the first appointment of the day generally assures prompt attention. On that particular morning, however, the kids' school bus failed to show up, and at 8:45, I was compelled to herd them into the car for a ten-minute round trip to the school. Returning home, I dumped Georgie unceremoniously into her carrier and raced to the vet's, walking in the door promptly at 9:00. "We'll be with you in a few minutes," the receptionist announced, turning her attention to the suited gentleman who had followed me into the office carrying a sample case. Probably a drug salesman, I concluded, seating myself reluctantly in the waiting area with the distressed cat meowing nervously beside me. Well, he wouldn't have to wait long, I thought, since innoculating Georgie would only take a minute. At 9:05, however, the salesman was ushered into an examining room, and I heard the doctor enter the room through a rear door. He and the salesman then embarked upon a perfectly audible perusal of new products, which promised to be lengthy.

"Excuse me, Miss," I addressed the receptionist, "but I had a nine o'clock appointment. Do I understand that the doctor is seeing the salesman who just dropped in? And if so, do you think that's right?" Though surprised, she interrupted the sales meeting and conveyed my displeasure to the vet, who appeared immediately and administered the needed injection to Georgie in the anticipated half-minute. I thanked him civilly enough and departed.

Case in Point: For a week or two, I had noticed the unmistakable twinge of a minor cavity in a rear molar. Though I was not yet in dire need of having my teeth cleaned, I decided that it would be efficient to have the cleaning done at the same time I had the cavity filled. I called a dentist to make an appointment, explaining what I wanted. "Oh, I couldn't schedule a prophylaxis and a filling at the same time," the secretary announced. "What if you didn't show up? We'd waste both the hygienist's and the doctor's time!"

"Thanks anyway, then," I replied. "I'm unwilling to schedule two separate appointments because you're afraid I might be a no-show, so I believe I'll find a dentist who has a bit more faith in his or her patients." The very next dentist I telephoned cheerfully agreed not only to take care of both the cavity and the cleaning in one sitting, but to schedule me after 5:00 P.M. or on Saturday morning, if that was more convenient.

Case in Point: After ten years of service above and beyond, our washing machine expired one Sunday morning. The prospect of waiting five work days, since I then worked outside my home, to accept delivery of a new machine the following weekend was unthinkable, as anyone with two active kids can verify, but the only alternative offered by the first appliance store I called was to take half a day off from work to await delivery on a weekday. No, they could not be more specific as to time. "Thanks anyway," I delivered the now familiar litany, "but I'm not willing to chain myself to the house for half a day because you can't schedule a specific delivery time." Two calls later, I ordered a new Maytag from Bernie's Appliance, whose delivery men would not only install the new machine and take away the old one at any reasonable day and hour I specified, but would do so while I was at work, if I preferred to leave a key. (They were bonded.) Bernie got my business that day, and he got it half a year later when the dryer bit the dust, too.

Who waits for whom is a basic power issue in any relationship, be it employer/employee, marriage, or vendor/consumer. Years ago, when I was secretary to the CEO of a supermarket chain, I was both annoyed and amused at the limits to which this jockeying for position was carried, particularly when it came to telephone calls. For no other reason than the accommodation of inflated egos, executives' secretaries were continually called upon to "get So-and-so on the line." The secretary would place the call, getting another executive's secretary on the line. Thence would ensue a lengthy negotiation as to which secretary would actually put the call through to her boss before the other got on the line. The executive who found himself talking to a secretary who said, "Just a moment, please, for Mr. Zroodlemex," lost the round.

Recognizing, at last, the absurdity and inefficiency of such mind games, even highly placed executives place and answer their own telephone calls on the spot these days, but the waiting game continues in other arenas, just as irritatingly. Like disarmament talks between politically opposed countries, the negotiations between those who keep others, and those who are kept, waiting are tricky. Basically, it's a matter of mutual respect; and until women value themselves and their roles as much as we value the roles of men in our society, insisting on the same punctuality from them that we jump through hoops to achieve, we cannot expect them to reciprocate. This lack of self-worth is an unattractive and unproductive posture that reinforces the domestic double standard every day.

Another of my pet nuisances is the persistently sexist assumptions made by others about Wayne's and my respective spheres of responsibility. Anything to do with the house or the kids, they assume, Judi handles. Anything to do with the finances or the cars, Wayne covers. Even when Wayne answers the telephone, the PTA representatives will ask to speak to me before requesting cookies for the school bake sale; and despite the fact that all accounts are in both of our names, the bank's congratulatory letters on our prompt pay-off of a loan are invariably addressed to Mr. Sprankle. Again, the only solution is matter-of-fact assertiveness. A nasty letter to the bank president saying, in effect, "Listen, Dummy. My salary was just as important as Wayne's to paying off the car loan, so shape up!" is unlikely to encourage a nonsexist approach in the future, but a polite reminder to the manager of the Customer Service Department that we prefer to be considered jointly responsible for such obligations might just do the trick. Likewise, Wayne's snide reference to the fact that I haven't baked a cookie since 1974 will probably not set a positive tone for future conversations with the PTA, but his expressed willingness to take care of whatever the problem is might get the point across.

In fairness, I recognize that the great majority of these people are merely acting according to their more traditional orientation to the division of domestic labor, and especially when it comes to older generations, I'm not going to challenge them. It's not their preferences that annoy me, after all—it's their insistence on foisting those preferences on me, which makes it all the harder for me to make a dent in the domestic double standard in the eyes of my children. If the PTA always calls Mom, and the bank always calls Dad, how can they help but draw inappropriate conclusions.

It is therefore well worthwhile, in my opinion, to see to it that somehow, some way, our efforts to share *all* domestic chores are clearly communicated to all those with whom we share our days. Aside from housework and direct, daily child care, these chores include entertaining the children's friends, supervising their extracurricular activities, and hosting family social events.

Because Wayne is rarely home before 6:00 P.M. on a weekday, it falls to me to transport and supervise Rick and Jenna's after-school visitors Monday through Friday. Since I have a notoriously low noise/clutter threshold and my work requires uninterrupted quiet, I find this irksome, but the kids have a right to entertain their friends, just as I have the right to welcome mine. To offset this imbalance in our respective roles, Wayne often takes over the role of host parent on the weekends while I work. Because he is relatively unbothered by either noise or clutter, I really thinks he makes the more congenial host, in fact. While I spend most of the time my kids' friends are in the house waiting impatiently for them to leave, Wayne can calmly pursue his latest woodworking or maintenance project, nearly oblivious to the confusion around him. And when, as infrequently as I can manage it, the kids have sleep-over guests, Wayne sleeps upstairs with the ruckus, while I collapse on the convertible sofa in the family room. I do, however, rise at dawn to cook the festive breakfast, while he catches an extra hour of sleep in relative peace.

When Rick entered Cub Scouts two years ago, I agreed on the condition that Wayne, not I, would supervise most of the required projects and would attend the monthly pack meetings, which are held at 7:00 P.M. on Thursday evenings. As with most of the children's activities, this arrangement still left plenty for me to do, and I assumed responsibility for Rick's uniform—a seemingly endless project involving the sewing on of dozens of badges, numbers, and other insignia—and for his attendance at weekly after-school den meetings. Although Wayne's unpredictable schedule has required me to sit through more monthly pack meetings than I originally bargained for, the Cub Scout officials know that Rick's participation is jointly facilitated by Wayne and by me—and so does Rick.

Jenna, too, is aware that Daddy is as likely as Mommy to transport her to her Saturday gymnastics class and that either of us is subject to weekend work. Wayne is just as acceptable as I am when it comes to accompanying her on a shopping trip for new clothes. In fact, he is far more likely to indulge her in an ice-cream cone on the way home. It also bothers her not one whit to see her large, masculine father waiting in the pink-and-chrome anteroom of the local beauty parlor while she gets her hair trimmed. One parent or the other—it's all the same to her.

Sunday school is another children's activity we've approached untraditionally. Both Wayne and I are agnostic, despite the comprehensive religious education both of us received as children. Our parents philosophically concluded that they did the best they could to expose us to Christian doctrine, and if it didn't take, so be it. Likewise, while neither of us desires strongly that our children develop an abiding faith in an almighty deity, we decided a couple of years ago that an exposure to Christian theology was something we wanted for our kids for reinforcement of our teachings about how other human beings should treat one another. As Norman Levinson, the senior pastor of the Congregational church we eventually selected, put it so well, we may not accept all of the church's answers, but we find it uplifting to be around people who are, at least, asking the questions.

In a letter to Dr. Levinson, I stated our position. Though we would not be able, for philosophical reasons, to join the church officially, we were entirely willing to assume our fair share of the church's expenses in exchange for our children's religious education. To his credit, Dr. Levinson responded warmly and promptly, applauding our honesty and our wish to give our children a chance to make their own decisions at appropriate ages. In a humorous postscript, he added that some of his best friends were agnostic!

From that point on, it was a matter of scheduling, since both Wayne and I tend to work on weekends. So, we decided to alternate. One week Wayne takes the children, usually attending church himself. The next week, I take my turn, sometimes sitting through the service if Dr. Levinson is speaking, sometimes dropping the kids off and going to the grocery store. Once in a great while, the four of us show up together, particularly when the kids are singing or putting on a holiday play. I have a feeling that our alternating appearances have led most of the congregation to conclude that Wayne and I are divorced, but it works for us.

While it's only natural to feel uneasy about such unconventional approaches to the supervision of children's activities and other domestic duties, if we ever hope to abolish the double standard it's important that women overcome their tendency to conform to what's expected of them by others. Whether we work at home or outside the home, during normal business hours or hours that suit our particular needs and rhythms, we must insist that our time is as valuable as anyone else's and defend our right not to give that time away to commitments that don't please us. This, of course, means learning how to say no, though it is not always possible to do so without giving—or having someone else take—offense.

I believe that the least offensive "No" is an impersonal "No." That is, it reflects a general policy instead of a specific response to a particular person's request. For example, Barbara, a university administrator of my acquaintance, found that it was becoming impossible to complete lengthy assignments at the office because her colleagues and subordinates enjoyed her company and were continually interrupting her to chat. Rather than snapping, "I've got work to do—please leave!" at individuals who dropped by at awkward times, which inevitably would have hurt their feelings, she suggested at a staff meeting that the office adopt a two-hour "quiet time" between 1:00 and 3:00 P.M. each afternoon, during which no calls or drop-in visitors would be permitted except in case of a genuine emergency. Her suggestion was greeted enthusiastically, and she gained the time she needed to complete her work in peace without offending anyone. In fact, the productivity of the entire staff improved greatly.

Since I work at home, telephone interruptions are a real nuisance. Even though my number is unlisted, I get a certain number of sales calls, plus calls from friends and relatives who feel free to call me during business hours at home, though they wouldn't dream of doing so were I at an outside office. To handle this headache as diplomatically as possible, I recorded a special message tape for my answering machine which indicates that I do not, as a general rule, accept routine calls until after 3:30 P.M. on weekdays, but callers may feel free to leave a message. In this way, I'm communicating a standard policy I've adopted to protect my working time, not refusing to speak to a particular person. In case of an emergency, my husband, mother, and children know to call and let the phone ring twice, hang up, and call back immediately. When I hear that pattern I drop everything and take the call.

Another problem to which I've taken an unconventional approach is that of door-to-door salespeople, religious representatives, and collectors for charitable organizations. I suppose a brusque "No Solicitors" sign on the door would suffice, but I have composed a little message that gets the point across without making me out to be quite such a grouch and posted it above the front doorbell. It reads, "No salespersons, religious representatives, or charities, please. We contribute annually to the charities of our choice and prefer not to be solicited personally. Thank you!" When I first posted this notice some years ago, it was not uncommon to greet guests at the door and find them studying my message carefully—probably to find out if they were welcome! Though I took a great deal of ribbing about my rather offbeat approach, most visitors soundly endorsed the idea. My mother went so far as to request a copy for her own front door, which I was happy to supply. "Does it work?" is what people really want to know, and for the most part, yes, it does. Of course, when some earnest child appears at my door, oblivious to the written word before him, I don't slam the door in his face. I just drop some change into the profferred container and wave goodbye. No system is foolproof.

Even the best of friends can be a nuisance at times, especially those whose internal clocks don't mesh with mine. While I'm at my peak in the afternoon, I've learned the hard way that most of my friends are night owls, ready to paint the town when I'm ready to collapse.

My own internal clock was set years ago when Ricky and Jenna were very young and I was employed at a full-time job that began at 8:15 A.M. in the city. The kids were always early risers, and I became accustomed to waking at 5:30 to prepare their breakfast, do a load of laundry, make beds, get the kids dressed, and do my own hair and make-up before leaving the house at 7:30 to take them to day-care and myself to work. Because I also happen to need a good deal of sleep, I'm always in bed by 10:00 P.M.—sometimes sooner, if I can manage it.

Though the children now often sleep until 7:00 A.M., my natural pattern remains unchanged, and I still do not function well in the evening. A social engagement that lasts past midnight is, for me, an ordeal, and I prefer not to go out on weeknights at all. This is hard for my friends to accept, and they keep trying to convert me into a night person. One woman in particular, whom I'll call Karen, used to be downright pesty in this regard. Though I love her dearly and truly enjoy her company, she persisted in inviting me out on weeknights, though I can't ever remember having accepted. I had given her every socially acceptable excuse in the book without her taking the slightest notice. In fact, she began countering my increasingly feeble parries with more aggressive thrusts. If I begged off on the basis that I didn't know if Wayne would be available to be with the kids, she would insist that her teenage daughter could babysit. If I murmured something vague about car trouble, she would insist on driving. If I said one of the kids seemed to be coming down with something, she would pooh-pooh me. Finally, I had enough. "No, thanks, Karen," I said flatly one evening. "Please don't misunderstand my refusal, but I get up very early in the morning, and I prefer not to go out on weeknights." To my surprise, she said she understood, and why hadn't I mentioned it before? Why hadn't I, indeed? Now, our visits are likely to consist of a Saturday morning chat over coffee, which works out well for both of us.

I guess I floundered for so long with Karen because I know it's disconcerting to be on the receiving line of a firm "No," as I had occasion to remember recently. In the course of doing research for an article, I approached a woman I know rather well, asking if she would be willing to allow me to interview her. When I followed my written enquiry with a telephone call, I was jolted when she turned me down flat. "No, I really don't want to get into it," she announced. "I've just got too many things to do already, and I keep saying yes when I should be saying no." It was hard for me not to take her refusal personally, but I realized, after thinking it over, that she had done the absolutely right thing. The working mother of two active children—and a talented aspiring playwright, to boot—she could not hope to carve out time for her creative work if she kept giving it away to support the work of others, like me. "Good for her," I concluded, and meant it.

Sometimes actions speak louder than words, and friends who refused to believe that Wayne and I are incapable of having a good time after 11:00 P.M. had to acknowledge the truth when they forced the issue. One couple with whom we socialize three or four times a year thought our expressed preference for a quick dinner and an early movie was a joke for years. Finally, they insisted that we join them for dinner at a seaside restaurant some forty miles from home. Things started out well. Bob and Linda picked us up, and we enjoyed a leisurely drive to the restaurant through the summer evening. Unfortunately, the restaurant was exceptionally crowded and our eight o'clock reservation wasn't honored until nearly nine. The service wasn't all that great, either, so it was nearly eleven before we finished dinner and re-entered the car for the return trip. Wayne and I were in the back seat, and we were on the road less than ten minutes before Wayne fell soundly asleep. I struggled to keep my eyes open and carry on a conversation, but there was no way to ignore the 200 pounds of sleeping man beside me.

Unfazed, Bob and Linda suggested dinner and a movie at a nearby shopping mall on another occasion. When we finished our pasta, however, the 8:00 P.M. showing of the film we wanted to see was sold out. Over our protests, Bob and Linda insisted that we have a drink, do a little window shopping, and return for the ten o'clock showing. By the time we finally entered the movie theater, I was yawning madly, what with the big meal and extra drink in my stomach, and I proceeded to sleep through *Romancing the Stone,* a lively, entertaining film I much enjoyed months later when it turned up on HBO one evening. After two disastrous outings, Bob and Linda finally accepted our preference for early evenings, and we have enjoyed many a Saturday afternoon barbecue or pizza-and-Trivial-Pursuit evening with them since then.

If I had to name my all-time, top-of-the-list nuisance, it would be houseguests, particularly in light of the domestic double standard which dictates that the bulk of the responsibility for overnight visitors fall on the woman of the house. Luckily, both Wayne's and my families live just minutes from us, so we are spared the agony of frequent, extended visits from relatives and in-laws. Still, we have put many out-of-state friends up for a night or two often enough that I have enormous sympathy for others who engage in this masochism regularly. For one thing, I can't imagine having more than one evening's conversation to offer anyone, which makes a three-day visit virtually impossible to sustain. For another, having a non-family member in the house makes me feel as though I have to be "on" all the time, constantly alert to a wish for food or drink, or entertainment. Then, of course, there's the substantial amount of cooking, cleaning, laundering, and what have you that overnight guests prompt.

I am told by those more experienced in the art of surviving houseguests that my approach is all wrong, and I'm sure they're right. Sandy tells me that when her mother-in-law arrives for her annual week-long visit, she insists that her husband, not she, be the one to arrange time off from work to entertain his mother while she carries on with the usual family game plan. "I just go right along doing my thing," she says cheerfully. "If Wilma is up when I'm making breakfast for the kids before work, I'll pour her a cup of coffee, but that's about it. She knows where everything is, and she also knows that I have a job to get to, and she's perfectly capable of serving herself. During the work week, life goes along pretty much as usual. I make sure I sit down and have a cup of tea or a glass of wine with Wilma when I get home from the office, but after that, I've got to get on with dinner. She's usually very happy to help. In fact, if she and Bill haven't gone out for the afternoon, she might even start dinner for me." Instead of making her mother-in-law feel like an imposition or a burden, Sandy maintains, including her in the normal family routine makes her feel like a welcome addition to the household. "Wilma would hate it if I waited on her hand and foot—not that I'm about to!" I think Sandy's onto something here.

Carmella, a busy literary agent, agrees. Even when overnighters aren't family members, she says, they prefer to be treated as if they are. "If they're good enough friends to be sleeping in your house," she suggests, "it's a safe bet that they'll enjoy being treated like members of the family. It's awkward to have somebody hovering over you all the time, wringing their hands and worrying that you're comfortable. In addition to having houseguests frequently, I often visit friends out of state for two or three days at a time when I'm traveling on business, and I hate it when they act like their homes are hotels. My favorite host is the one who says, 'Food's in the kitchen, liquor's in this cabinet, and the towels are in the hall closet. Make yourself at home!' and allows me to do exactly that. I'm a big girl, and if I really need something, I'll ask!"

Accommodating houseguests once they arrive is one thing, but how do you fend off friends and relatives who invite themselves into your home? Not having this problem myself, I again turned to others for advice. The consensus: Make your preferences crystal clear long before the problem ever comes up. "I hate being a houseguest, and I hate having them," says Bonnie firmly, "and I make sure everybody knows it. Whenever someone tells me that they're either going to visit someone else or are having houseguests themselves, I say just that, loudly. I figure by this time, I must have said it to everybody I know a dozen times, so the problem never arises at our house! Once, friends invited me to visit them at the Cape. I accepted, but I added that I preferred to stay at a nearby motel. When they protested that they had plenty of room, why pay for a motel, I just told them straight out that I didn't enjoy being a houseguest. Once they understood that I wasn't being a martyr to avoid imposing on them but was simply accommodating a personal preference, they didn't press me. In fact, I think they were really rather relieved, and our visit was a great success."

How about a houseguest who appears to have moved in permanently? "If you find yourself in that fix," Bonnie argues, "you've brought it on yourself. If you're rash enough to invite someone to stay in your home, the very least you should do is extend the invitation for a specific period of time and make certain you have a sure-fire excuse ready to get out of extending it. You could say something like, 'How about coming for the weekend? We'll be glad to drop you back at the airport Monday morning because we're going there anyway to pick up Hal's mother and her two unhousebroken St. Bernards that morning.' That's a little far-fetched, but you get the general idea."

Whatever the circumstances, these women agreed that whoever did the inviting should bear the bulk of the entertainment burden, including the cooking and the cleaning. "When my parents are in town, I do the hostessing. When Fred's mother is in town, he does the cooking, or we go out to dinner. That way, there's something in a visit from my mother-in-law that even I can enjoy!" chuckles a woman who, understandably, prefers to remain anonymous!

However a woman decides to deal with the little nuisances that are an integral part of daily life, she will do so more effectively if she acquires the habit of straightforward, honest communication with those around her. There will always be some people who will view untraditional approaches to traditional problems as unacceptable, but it has been my experience that there are far more who will openly or secretly applaud an honest attempt to change what needs changing in our lives in whatever way works best for us.

By making our preferences known, insisting that

others accord us the same respect they want from us, valuing our time as much as we value theirs, and refusing to conform just to make others more comfortable with our behavior, we can extend our efforts to abolish the domestic double standard outside our homes as well as in them.

Not even the longest running family tradition is immutable. A little frank communication can turn up some surprising results—and go a long way toward easing the domestic double standard.

TRIBAL CUSTOMS

WHEN I WAS A CHILD, I looked forward to holidays for the same reasons that children have always looked forward to holidays—presents, sugary treats forbidden at other times, and a respite from the dreary routines of school. But even then, I acknowledged the less enjoyable aspects of "special" days, which included uncomfortable, dressy clothes, visits to unfavorite relatives, and more often than not, an extra sermon at church. Still, on balance, I anticipated holidays as a child with pleasure.

Once I became a mother—that is, the provider of the presents and sugary treats and the primary care-giver for overexcited children on prolonged hiatus from school—the cons of holidays soon outweighed the pros in my mind. Though it took years for me to admit it, I began anticipating Christmas, Thanksgiving, Easter, family birthdays, and other days of ritual throughout the year with the same exuberance with which Marie Antoinette must have awaited her beheading—and even so, *she* didn't have to go through the ordeal half a dozen times a year, every year.

Recently I've noticed a significant waning of enthusiasm for holidays among my working-mom colleagues, too. From time to time, we have discussed why this is so. It is partly the extra work involved, which ranges from minimal to mind-boggling, depending on which festive occasion looms. For some, it is partly the hypocrisy of participating in religious rites in which we no longer believe and in childhood fantasies we have long outgrown. For example, I know lots of families who attend church only on Christmas and Easter. When I ask why they bother, the response is generally a shrugged, "Custom, I guess." And for people like me, the charade of a rabbit who delivers dyed, hard-boiled eggs is pretty difficult to sustain, especially when you're on a low-cholesterol diet.

Too, there is always the annoying materialism associated with major holidays such as Christmas, which overwhelms every effort to celebrate an old fashioned holiday in the spirit of giving to those less fortunate than we with a steadily mounting, advertisement-induced greed in our children. Every December, I wish fervently that the television set would break down, but even if I got lucky, the kids would probably just add a 25-inch Sony to their interminable "gimme" lists. The whole syndrome inspires huge guilt in us parents, torn as we are between our desire to indulge our children and our awareness of those who are in genuine need as we plunk down $59.95 for a Lego block kit against our better judgment.

My growing disenchantment with holidays was fed also by the expectations of relatives and in-laws that I would fall obediently in with their customs, cast in stone years earlier. Did they never consider that I might have a few customs I wished to honor on holidays myself? Perhaps most of all, I came to resent society's mandates that I feel festive according to the calendar even if it killed me—an extension of the insistence by salesclerks that I "have a nice day," which never fails to raise my hackles.

A quick survey among the mothers attending a recent career workshop confirmed my suspicion that I'm not alone in my holiday hostility. "I hate holidays," stated

Marge, the mother of three, without hesitation. She paused, then amended, "Actually, I love Christmas, but Ed's mother makes even that absolutely miserable. His family never developed strong holiday traditions, but Mrs. Mason is always trying to fit in somewhere and say, 'You're not doing it the right way.'

"I used to love Thanksgiving, too," Marge continued, on a roll. "My family would always sing, 'We Gather Together' before we ate dinner at my sister's, and we'd go for a walk after the meal, and it was just fun. When we were younger, we'd always do a Thanksgiving play or a show. While the parents were sitting around drinking coffee and eating pie, we kids would go and make up a play and then come back and present it. Then the grandchildren started doing it, and it became a tradition."

It was a tradition that proved to be short lived, unfortunately. "When Ed and I were married, Mrs. Mason announced that in twenty-two years of being married, she had always had Thanksgiving at her house, and she expected us to come there, too. Because it's just the two of them, my mother-in-law and her husband, we felt we had to start going there. They really don't have anybody else. We're the family, and that's it. I've adjusted to it, but it's not a fun holiday anymore."

Christmas has deteriorated in much the same way, with Marge sacrificing many of her preferences and customs in deference to her mother-in-law. "My family always used to have a traditional ethnic Christmas. We'd have the seven meatless dishes on Christmas Eve, and the kids would open their presents from the family that night. Then Mrs. Mason would say, 'Oh, you have to come here on Christmas Eve,' and it got to be a real push-pull situation. Finally, I compromised by inviting the Masons to our house on Christmas Eve, and then on Christmas Day, they would be invited to the home of whoever in my family had the Christmas meal. It's just something I have to live with, I guess. I can't imagine how it could be changed, because I wouldn't hurt my mother-in-law, and I know she would be hurt if we didn't fall in with her expectations. One year, we didn't go to her house for Thanksgiving, and she was devastated. She cried! 'For the first time in thirty-five years, I didn't make a turkey,' she said. She really felt terrible. Our kids are her only grandchildren, and that makes a difference, of course. When my father-in-law retired, they were talking about moving to Florida, but they didn't go because they didn't want to be away from their grandchildren. It's not as if they live through them, or anything. They just enjoy them."

The expectations of grandparents have more than a little to do with our growing irritation with major holidays. This is not exactly a new development, of course. What is new is that the majority of today's wives and mothers hold full-time jobs outside the home in addition to performing the bulk of the household work, a fact we might reasonably expect to have acknowledged by older generations in our families with appropriate compromises at holiday time. Unfortunately, this doesn't often happen spontaneously; but sometimes it is possible to start the ball rolling without triggering a family feud.

Before Wayne and I became parents, I mostly gritted my teeth and endured holidays as the price of a committed, long-term relationship, even though the proliferation of occasions in his large, midwestern family annoyed me more and more. Wayne has a brother and three sisters, all married, all with at least two children, all living within five miles of us and of Louise, Wayne's mother. As time passed, the usual holidays were augmented by wedding and baby showers for a seemingly endless parade of cousins, nieces, and nephews' fiancées; birthdays, anniversaries, and a mid-summer all-family barbecue. Preceding each of these events, it was I, not Wayne, who shopped for food and a gift, prepared the required casserole or gelatin mold, wrapped the present, and selected an appropriate card. All he was expected to do was show up, and when it came to the showers, he didn't even have to do that!

Whatever horrors preceded it, Christmas was always

the capper, even Before Children. Living only a few miles from both sets of parents meant we didn't have to do any long-distance holiday traveling, thank heaven; but on the minus side of the ledger, our proximity to both of our families involved us automatically in everyone's plans. And so, Christmas became an endurance marathon—eighteen hours of too much food and drink, and too much time in overheated, poorly ventilated quarters with too many people, interspersed with hurried trips between my parents' house and Wayne's parents' house. It was awful, but it wasn't nearly as awful as it got after Ricky was born.

Arriving as he did on November 19, and colicky as he was from day one, it is not, in retrospect, surprising that my firstborn triggered my holiday rebellion. I have a dim recollection of Christmas Eve 1975, the day on which I realized fully the Christmas repercussions of having borne a child. When he came into the world, Rick had ten cousins. (The number is now somewhere around twenty, what with a fifteen-year age spread among the first cousins, several of whom are now the parents of his second cousins. Frankly, I lost count years ago.) At that time, custom required each Sprankle to give every other Sprankle in his or her relative category a gift, and it dawned on me that, by virtue of my recent initiation to motherhood, I was suddenly responsible for purchasing and wrapping ten additional gifts to distribute at Grandma Louise's the next day.

I had slept very little during the preceding four weeks, and my grip on sanity was tenuous, at best—but that terrible realization really threw me. I went nuts. Wayne was, as usual, traveling on business, so I vented my rising hysteria on his brother Kip, instead. "I can't do it!" I shrieked at him via telephone. "I won't!" I have no memory of his response, which I'm sure was both amused and sympathetic. I do recall that I did not then, or ever, purchase Christmas gifts for each of my children's cousins.

Instead of creating ill will among my in-laws, my outburst apparently served as a needed catalyst for change within the family, the others members of which were entirely receptive to my suggestion, in a more diplomatic moment, that each cousin and each aunt/uncle couple draw the name(s) of one other in that category for whom to purchase a Christmas gift. We even agreed on dollar limits for each gift category to eliminate any hard feelings when gifts were compared. This eminently sane amendment to the Christmas madness had a number of positive results: Each family had far fewer presents to select and wrap, of course. Because each gift was more thoughtfully chosen, it was far more likely to be genuinely appreciated. And the move took hours off the traditional one-at-a-time gift-opening ceremony on Christmas Day!

While not as dramatic, other changes have occurred for the good in our approach to holidays. Before sharing them, let me say that my side of the family has always been small. I have only one sister, who is married but who has opted not to have children, and my mother, who was widowed several years ago. Even when Dad was alive, holidays were not a big deal, probably because my mother went through worse than I did when she was first married. My paternal grandfather was a church choirmaster and schoolteacher. When Mom married into the family, she was given the horrendous task each year of buying and wrapping some 200 gifts for the choir members and school children in addition to serving the holiday meal to some fifty relatives. Sometime before my tenth birthday, Mom, too, had a holiday rebellion, which was somewhat less amicably received among the members of Dad's family. After that, we spent holidays mostly at home, quietly acknowledging the day among ourselves, except for Thanksgiving, which we celebrated in the fanciest restaurant we could find!

At any rate, Mom, Penny and her husband Eric, and I are not what I would call wet blankets, but we do resist the idea of contrived festivity, which is how I look upon major holidays. Left alone, we would probably agree to ignore the hoop-dee-doo, but circumstances—well, let's face it, my kids—have thrust it upon us. Grandma Polly, Aunt

Penny, and Uncle Eric are as essential a part of the kids' holiday as are the more amenable Sprankles, so for their sakes, my family rallies. We have, however, arrived at a plan with which we can all live.

First, since I live one mile from my mother and Penny lives 100 miles away, we have agreed to ignore all holidays except Thanksgiving and Christmas. Every now and then Penny will drive up from Ridgefield and take Mom and me to lunch, or Eric and Penny will have us down there for a poolside picnic, but those things are spontaneous, and therefore fun, so they don't count here. I'm talking strictly about annual rituals.

Next, because we also live one mile from Wayne's mother, who absolutely expects us to be actively involved in major holidays, Wayne and I have had to come to terms. On Thanksgiving, which I'm pleased to say I once again enjoy, my sister and her husband meet Wayne and me and the kids at Mom's house late in the morning, where everybody visits for half an hour, tops. Wayne then takes our kids to his mother's for Thanksgiving dinner, while Eric treats my mother, my sister, and me to an elegant, tranquil restaurant meal. I do not appear at my mother-in-law's house on Thanksgiving any longer, but as long as her son and grandchildren are there, she is content. It works out superbly! Instead of arriving home overfed and frazzled at day's end, the kids feel properly feted, without me glowering at them all day. Both Wayne and I feel we have fulfilled our family obligations satisfactorily, so we have no guilt trips to endure. Wayne gets to watch his football games while all the cousins trample each other in his mother's back yard. And Penny and Eric, who, after all, decided not to have children, do not have to endure interminable hours with mine.

Then comes Christmas. This is admittedly a more complicated holiday, but we have found ways to make it manageable. I have already mentioned our name-drawing strategy to keep the gift list within reason. The next major hurdle is scheduling.

When you have young children, there is no way to avoid their awakening at dawn on Christmas. In another ten years, we may be allowed to snooze until a decent hour, but not yet. Fortunately, our church holds a lovely 7:30 P.M. service on Christmas Eve. It is centered around the children's nativity play and the traditional music of Christmas, which we all enjoy. It sets a nice tone for the coming day, and the service ends early enough to allow everyone to get to bed at a reasonable hour, regardless of how long they actually sleep; and as soon as the kids are safely stashed in their beds, Wayne and I arrange their presents under the tree and—this is very important—hang their filled stockings on their doorknobs. This tactic probably gains us an extra half hour of sleep on Christmas morning, since the kids jump into one or the other of their beds and explore their stockings before descending to the first floor for the main event.

Another of our strategies is not to exchange Christmas gifts between ourselves, which may strike some as cold. It really isn't. Instead of adding to the confusion on that day, we treat each other to something special before or after . . . an overnight excursion to New York for a couple of Broadway shows and dinner, a new stereo system, a video cassette recorder, or new family room furniture, for example. This way, Christmas morning is truly the kids' time, and we can concentrate on assembling things, installing batteries, explaining game rules, and what have you.

After a breakfast of coffee-cake and orange juice, everyone helps clean up the first round of clutter and gets into presentable, but comfortable, clothes to await the arrival of Aunt Penny and Uncle Eric, who pick up my mother on their way to Newington from Ridgefield. When the car is unloaded, we all once again enjoy ogling the impressive pile of packages under the tree while a couple of bottles of excellent champagne, contributed by Eric, chill in the freezer. When greedy curiosity overwhelms us, we indulge in a wild hour of paper-ripping and champagne sipping while passing the camera around. It's an orgy that never fails to satisfy, since we are careful to exchange wish lists well in advance of the official Christmas shopping season.

Because Penny and Eric treat me at Thanksgiving, I do the honors for Christmas dinner, which I keep simple and plentiful to allow for lots of wonderful leftovers, and thus no cooking, over the next few days. Most of the meal is prepared in advance, especially the pumpkin and apple pies, which Mrs. Smith or Sara Lee do far better in their commercial kitchens than I could from scratch. An elegant roast of pork or beef is simply a matter of finding a good butcher and setting the oven timer, and a tossed salad takes maybe ten minutes to fix. I add some fresh, crusty rolls, which require all of five minutes in the toaster oven; a couple of vegetables prepared the night before and reheated with the rolls; and that's it. Even the table gets set the night before, prior to leaving for the 7:30 church service—unless we have kittens in the house, as we did last year, with interesting results by morning.

By mid-afternoon, my family departs, and Wayne and I spend half an hour loading the dishwasher and redistributing the unwrapped presents to the appropriate bedrooms. If we're lucky, we might even snatch a few minutes with our feet up before we move into the third and final phase of Christmas at his mother's house.

We are tired by this time, but there is light at the end of the tunnel. Aunts and uncles chat congenially while the older children try out their new games and tots nod peacefully on any available shoulder. After the gifts are exchanged, everyone over the age of sixteen pitches in with cleanup, taking turns washing and drying, taking out trash, and putting away leftovers from the buffet earlier in the day. Soon, the parents of younger children make their goodnights, and the room grows relatively peaceful. By 7:30, we too are on our way home with another Chirstmas safely behind us.

Yes, it's a marathon, but I have come to enjoy it. For one thing, the day as it is now structured has involved a number of important compromises, and most have been in my favor. I had always felt, in previous years, that my mother was entitled to have her children and grandchildren come to her on Christmas, but when I suggested that it was difficult for us to cart the kids around to both grandmothers every year, she quite happily agreed to join us at our house—in fact, I think she suggested it. This way, Mom's Christmas Day lasts about five hours, which is as much as she finds enjoyable anyway. It's fun, but she is glad, I think, to return to the tranquility of her own home after a hectic afternoon and not to have to deal with the dirty dishes, gift wrapping, and dismantling of the tree. My sister and her husband, who might justifiably ask us to travel to Ridgefield now and again for the holiday, recognize the extra work that Christmas with children entails and kindly do not begrudge the drive. They see that Mom gets safely here and back, and Wayne and I do dinner and the cleanup but don't have to travel. It's an acceptable trade-off. My mother-in-law has come to realize that it's difficult for all of her children and grandchildren to spend a major part of the day at her house, since everyone has in-laws to accommodate. So instead of insisting on a sit-down dinner, she has compromised by serving a buffet to which we all contribute a favorite dish, and everyone comes in and out as their other obligations permit. Finally, the whole show lasts just twenty-four hours, from Christmas Eve church service through the return trip from Grandma Louise's house, which makes it endurable. To their credit, nobody in the family has ever imposed on our Christmas Eve, leaving us free to enjoy an eggnog at the home of good friends who customarily hold an open house, or to entertain old friends who are in the area for Christmas with their parents.

The confining of Christmas to a twenty-four-hour period, so far as possible, was difficult, but worth it. For several years, I persisted with a holiday custom of our own, an elaborate open house on a Sunday between Thanksgiving and Christmas to which every guest brought one kind of cookie and left with an assortment of those brought by others. We decorated the house and the front porch, arranged for overflow parking, made gallons of hot mulled wine, hired a waitress to pass the hot hors d'oeuvres and someone to entertain the children in the basement rec room, baked dozens of cookies, sent out one hundred handwritten invitations, and generally made a Big Production out of it. Some years, the party seemed to be a hit, but more frequently, as the years went on, I noticed that the majority of those who attended seemed to be doing so to avoid offending us, for God's sake. They blew in, already exhausted from some seasonal happening or other, stayed the obligatory forty-five minutes, and then dashed off to yet another event on their crammed social calendars. Why, I finally thought, am I wearing myself out throwing a party no one really wants to attend at this time of year? Why not do everyone a favor, myself included, and just *stop*. And so, I did. The relief was exquisite—I may never throw another party again!"

Fewer holiday parties is a trend that seems to be catching on. For example, I've noticed that office parties are far less elaborate than they used to be—and far less likely to be command performances for spouses of employees. Wayne and his colleagues used to throw a restaurant-based party every year until we all admitted we weren't really looking forward to another two-hour-wait-until-dinner-is-served evening. Now the boys just go out for a couple of drinks somewhere before the holiday and leave it at that, which is wonderful, too!

Aside from major holidays, tribal customs such as weddings, baby showers, and engagement parties reinforce the domestic double standard. Traditionally, such occasions are designed for and by women, and because this is true, I find most of them uninteresting. When I was married, I refused all offers of a wedding shower, a move that was regarded by my prospective in-laws as aberrant behavior brought on by nerves. But when I declined a baby shower when I was pregnant with Ricky six years later, I was branded not only a maverick but a heretic. No baby shower, indeed! Unable to accept my simple, straightforward loathing for that type of gathering, my relatives decided I must be superstitious about accepting baby gifts before the infant had arrived safely, then simply waited for Rick's birth before presenting their lovely gifts. When I declined a shower yet again when expecting Jenna, they finally began to get the picture.

Declining to participate in wedding and baby showers for myself was one thing, but declining invitations to showers for others in the family was another, far trickier, matter. My objections, after all, were personal. If other women welcomed such fetes and were willing to undertake the work involved, would I not be surly to refuse to attend? Unsure of how others might interpret my refusals, I attended—for a few years, anway, until my perfunctory appearances and quick disappearances seemed to me to be even more ungracious than simply declining the invitations up front. Since the main point of all showers is the amassing of trousseaus and layettes, I decided to compromise. When the last of Wayne's nieces was married, I made it known through the family grapevine that while I would happily provide an appropriate gift on future such occasions, I would no longer attend showers. No hard feelings, please. Perhaps my in-laws had at last accustomed themselves to this strange creature in their midst, or perhaps I had been overly sensitive in anticipating their reaction to my pronouncement. Whichever, it appeared to ruffle no feathers, and I have been spared the necessity of getting all gussied up on a Sunday afternoon to sit for hours in some overcrowded living room, balancing a cup of black coffee on one knee and steadfastly refusing the calorie-laden goodies that abound while making boring small-talk about Disastrous Weddings and Incredibly Painful Births I have Known.

Children's birthday parties are another tribal custom in which the domestic double standard figures prominently, since mothers are usually the emcees on these occasions. Despite the overwhelming demands on our time and energy as we juggle at least two full-time roles, we are still somehow expected to provide the festivities on each anniversary of our children's births, and to send them off with appropriate gifts and attire to celebrate their friends' birthdays. Actually, I would quite enjoy celebrating the fact that I'm not doing this birthday what I was doing on my son's and daughter's *very* first birthday, but a children's party ain't my idea of a celebration.

At first, birthdays were relatively uncomplicated, a matter of inviting both grandmothers over to watch the birthday baby, perched importantly in a high chair, stuffing fistfuls of cake into his mouth. Wayne snapped a few pictures for the family album; I scraped the frosting off the kid, and that was about it until Rick, then Jenna, entered nursery school. Suddenly, birthdays became a Big Deal involving presents from the immediate family first thing in the morning; cupcakes or a sheet cake sent to school if, God forbid, the birthday fell on a weekday; invitations issued to as many as twelve school chums to whose parties *my* child had been previously invited; the scheduling of some elaborate sequence of events such as roller skating followed by cake and ice cream at home. After having delivered all the children to their homes, we would return to our own to face yet more cake and ice cream with grandmothers. Two years ago, when I found myself at a particularly nauseating "birthday party parlor" known as Chuck E. Cheese trying unsuccessfully to ride herd on a dozen overstimulated youngsters, I called a halt.

New Rule Number 1 is that each child's birthday is celebrated on one day and one day only. No more duplicate cakes are sent to school. If the real birthday falls on a school day, it is discreetly ignored until the following weekend unless a brief, after-school event is acceptable to the birthday child.

New Rule Number 2 is that a maximum of four children are invited to any birthday party. With Jenna and Rick, that makes six, which is as many children as I ever care to see in one place at one time. I discovered, you see, that the reason for inviting a dozen children was not to enjoy their company but to rake in more loot; so when we suggested that a more substantial gift might be forthcoming if we didn't have to expend so much feeding and entertaining all those kids, the new rule met with surprisingly little resistance.

Rule Number 3 states that the birthday child may select a preferred activity lasting no more than two hours, including transportation. On one occasion, Rick opted to take his sister and two of his best friends back to the loathsome Chuck E. Cheese, where they were free to play all the video games they could for exactly one hour. Without an uncontrollable mob to supervise, it really wasn't bad at all! Another time, Jenna chose a grown-up dinner with us and a special friend at a Polynesian restaurant that featured a hokey, but nonetheless entertaining, dinner show complete with hula dancers and a fire-eater. All in all, things are working out very well.

While I was congratulating myself for having regained control over an insane situation, I received a telephone invitation for Rick from the mother of one of his school friends. "We'd like to have Ricky join us for Joey's birthday," Helen began, "but please, don't have him bring a birthday present. We're doing birthdays a lot differently this year, trying to have the kids invite just a few of the friends they really enjoy to do something special for the afternoon. We're keeping it very low key." I burst out laughing and confided the details of my own rebellion, then applauded her for going me one better.

My neighbor Tina supports the new trend, too. "I hate birthday parties," she admits. "All these kids come in, and there's all this noise, and nobody seems to have a good time. Maybe they do, but I remember going to a lot of birthday parties when I was little. They were okay, but . . ." She wrinkles her nose. These days, she and her husband Bill are trying to get birthday parties for their three kids back to the way they used to be. "We used to have really nice, simple birthday parties when our first one, John, was little. Once, we rented a pony, and John had four of his good friends over, and we had a hot-dog roast. It was a very special day." She hopes to have more such special days in the future, with just a few good friends sharing in some activity all will remember.

In neither the immediate nor the extended family are tribal customs easily revised, but the effort to do so is often very worthwhile, and our expectations of resistance from other family members usually turn out to have been exaggerated (as I discovered, for example, when I suggested drawing names for the exchange of Christmas gifts among the Sprankles). Marsha, the mainstay of the word processing department in a corporation that employed me some years ago, first brought this to my attention. Marsha has been married nearly eighteen years, and she was candid about her resentment of always having to celebrate major holidays in her mother's home instead of her own. The custom had been established early on, when Marsha's mother had taken enormous satisfaction in cooking for a large crowd of appreciative relatives. The years went on with Marsha and her brothers and sisters bringing their families to her mother's house on Thanksgiving, Christmas, and Easter to allow Grandma to revel in the preparation of a huge feast. What they failed to consider was that Grandma's attitude might have changed.

One Christmas evening, as her mother fell exhausted into an armchair beside her, Marsha said, "Gee, Mom, you look so tired. I know how much you enjoy it, but I wish you'd let us help you more with the holiday cooking." To her astonishment, her mother responded, "Frankly, dear, I don't enjoy it nearly as much as I used to!" It was a revelation that led to a candid discussion among everyone present, greasing the wheels for a complete revamping of the family's holiday customs. Now holiday meals are prepared cooperatively and hosted in rotation by Marsha and her brothers and sisters. "Why I didn't touch base with Mom sooner, I'll never know," Marsha concluded. "I waited eighteen years before I opened my mouth. We thought we were the ones being imposed on to accommodate Mom's preferences, and all the time, she thought she was accommodating us. It just never occurred to us that her feelings might have changed.

It just goes to show you. Nothing—not even the longest running family tradition—is immutable. A little frank communication can turn up some surprising results—and go a long way, in some instances, toward easing the domestic double standard.

As any working mother will attest, there are times when no amount of advance planning and conscientious preparation can head off a hectic spell, but even then, there are ways to manage the seemingly unmanageable.

A QUESTION OF TIME

THOSE TIME/MOTION STUDY EXPERTS who were all the rage ten years ago could have learned a great deal about the efficient use of time by following a working mother around with a stopwatch for a day. It would have been easy to pick one out of the crowd. A working mother is that woman you see at red lights, writing out a check in her lap in preparation for her next stop while waiting for the green. She's the one bringing her checkbook register up to date in the dentist's waiting room. She's also the one who never puts a can or a box into her cart at the supermarket without first checking to be sure the price tag is on it. It's a question of time—because she hasn't got any to waste for a price check if the tag is missing. If a quick survey of the area doesn't turn up a woman exhibiting these behaviors, just look for a lady with a list in her hand. Lists are working mothers' links to sanity.

When I was growing up, my sister Penny was known affectionately as the family listmaker. Achievement oriented and highly organized, she made lists of everything—what to do, what to wear, who to call, homework assignments, you name it. I chuckled at her little eccentricity then, but during a particularly hectic period some years ago, I reached for a pencil and paper, furtively drew up a list, and have never looked back.

Prosaic though they may be, lists can be one of the most effective defenses against the domestic double standard. While we are drawing them up, they help us get organized and set priorities, and once they exist, they serve as effective reminders, offering the peace of mind of a hedged bet. Once a thing has been written down, it doesn't have to be retained in the conscious mind. It can drift quietly into the subconscious until a review of the list prompts us to recall it at the appropriate moment. Obviously, you do have to remember to look at the list, but it's a lot easier to get into the habit of perusing a list every morning over coffee, say, than to attempt to recall everything you promised two weeks ago to get purchased, dry-cleaned, painted, mended, or whatever, *today.* Best of all, once you've written it down, you can then delegate responsibility for following through on to *someone else.*

Kyle, the editor of a corporate house organ, says her work is an endless succession of deadlines, and she clings to her lists for dear life. During the work day, her priorities are set by a tickler file, which is a list on file cards instead of a single sheet of paper, arranged by date. The last thing Kyle does each day is to look at the cards filed behind the next day's date to fix tomorrow's priorities in her mind.

It's a habit she's carried over to her home life, in which she is the mother of two boys, aged ten and twelve, who are sports enthusiasts. "David plays soccer in the fall and pitches for his Little League team in the spring. Jerry does soccer and basketball. I really couldn't be happier about their interest in sports, because I think team playing is good for them physically and mentally. It does wreak havoc with our schedules, though, when we try to arrange transportation to and from all their practices and games on top of work and school, Hebrew school, medical and dental appointments, and so on. It's not like the teams always practice at one school, either. David can have two practices and a game in a single week, all at different locations, and Jerry can, too. That makes six discrete sets of information to remember that week alone in addition to whatever else crops up. If I didn't have a master calendar, I can easily picture myself driving from one schoolyard to the next, desperately trying to remember where one of them is."

The master calendar to which Kyle refers is a desk blotter-sized affair tacked firmly to the door leading from her kitchen into the garage, just steps away from the telephone. A sharp pencil hangs next to it on a string. "I keep the schedule in pencil," Kyle notes, "because things are always changing. It's hard to sort out old information from new when it's all crammed in together and crossed out and written over. This way, we just erase it and start over."

When the boys' team schedules are first issued, Kyle notes the time and location of each practice and game carefully on the calendar, then delegates the responsibility for entering changes to David and Jerry. "If they forget to change the calendar, I refuse to accept responsibility—and that's happened already. But when one of the kids misses a practice, his coach isn't likely to let him forget to change the calendar the next time around. Ten laps around the field is an effective reminder!"

As she does on the job, Kyle reviews the next day's events on the master calendar last thing each night, noting who must be where the following day. She then makes quick notes on those bright yellow note papers with a strip of light adhesive at the top—for her husband Mark and her sons. "If I know Mark has a 5:00 P.M. appointment in town and Jerry's practice ends at 6:30, I remind Mark to pick Jerry up on his way home. If David has a game at the North School, I know he'll be biking home past the 7-Eleven and can pick up the milk and bread on my shopping list. And if by some miracle we're all going to be free when one of the boys has a game, I'll remind everyone to keep it that way so we can go to see it as a family!"

Dedicated listmakers often keep notebooks of lists on long-range subjects. These might include headings such as "Monthly Heating Bills" to help plan next season's budget, "Car Maintenance" to assist in scheduling oil changes and tire rotation, and "Medical Expenses" to signal when the deductible has been met on the family's medical insurance. Other notebooks constitute wish lists with categories such as "Vacation Ideas" and "Restaurants" to keep good suggestions handy for when the budget will accommodate a long weekend or a night out. My friend Mary Ann has notebook pages for each of her four children on which they are invited to enter their most-wanted items for birthdays and Christmas. "That way," she says, "I'm never at a loss when their grandparents ask me for gift suggestions. I keep a page for Jack and me, too, just in case we win the Lottery!"

A realtor acquaintance, Alicia, who knows how important such a record can be when a house is up for sale, makes regular entries of all home improvements, noting the type of work done, the date, and the exact cost. "If you can show that you replaced the furnace in 1983, you can justify upping the asking price of the house by the cost at sale time," she notes. "Even painting and wallpapering are worth recording, since it can easily cost $200 or more to paper an average bedroom at today's prices." Accurate records of gas, heating oil, and electricity bills are also appreciated by buyers, since such expenses are often a determining factor in their decision to buy or not.

Marguerite, an avid gardener, keeps a list of flowering annuals and perennials in her notebook, "because I can never remember what did well last summer when the next planting time rolls around. If I keep a list, even Hank, who can't tell a marigold from a petunia, can come back with the right seedlings from the nursery." Her list also helps to remind her about the impatiens that wilted in full sunlight and the roses that drooped in the semi-shade of the maple tree last season.

Nancy, who loves to entertain friends at buffet dinners, keeps a list of prime party goodies and where to get them at a moment's notice. As I read her careful notations of which liquor store in town carries Moet & Chandon White Star Extra Dry champagne and where the tastiest pâté can be obtained, I understood why her parties are so successful and look so effortless. Despite her modest claim that she just throws something together at the last minute, I now know she plans well in advance exactly what that something will be.

Advance planning is integral to a working mother's time-management strategy. Though it is difficult enough to get through just one day at a time, thinking ahead has many potential benefits, not the least of which is involving other members of the family in future tasks. "If I leave everything until the last minute," says Clarisse, a dental hygienist, "I wind up doing it all myself, because it takes less time than trying to explain what needs doing to somebody else. But if I give some thought to what's coming up next week or next month, I have a chance to get Mike lined up to get the car in for the 50,000-mile service or to go in late one morning so he can get the kids in for their dental check-up before school. I used to take care of all those things myself, figuring it was easier than going through the hassle of asking Dave to change his schedule and so on, but I did feel as though it wasn't fair to my boss. Why should it always be him, not Dave's boss, who has to do without help because I have to leave early or go in late? If Dave has advance notice, there's no reason why he can't make those arrangements, too. One day, I was ready to leave for work when I remembered the kids were being dismissed early from school that afternoon, and I hadn't arranged for the time off. 'Damn it, why is it always me?' I shouted at Dave. 'Damn it, why don't you ever ask me?' he answered, and he called his boss on the spot and got the afternoon off with no problem."

Many women have been surprised by similar responses from their husbands, whom they rarely even bothered to ask to share in scheduling problems. I used to be among them. "So why," I inquired nastily of Wayne one evening after a go-round on this subject, "don't you ever just *do* things without waiting for me to *ask*? They're your kids, too, and your cars and your cats. You know what needs doing just as well as I do." But there, he had me.

"As a matter of fact, I don't," he shot back. "You're the one who goes through their school bags for notes and appointment reminders every day. You get home first and take the messages off the answering machine and take in the mail. You're the one who takes the phone calls between four and six-thirty when I get home. If you don't fill me in, how in hell am I supposed to know what's going on? I'm not a mindreader!"

I had to admit I'd assumed a rather martyred posture over the years, hanging grimly onto a perhaps unjustified resentment of Wayne's lack of involvement with daily scheduling problems. The spat prompted some hard thinking, and I reviewed the facts more objectively. Due to his work hours, it was true that he was generally unavailable to field the input on scheduled activities, and without my output, there was really no way he could get in on the act. "But you never remember what I tell you anyway," was my last feeble argument.

"Write it down," he rejoined coolly, and so I did. Adopting Kyle's adhesive note papers, I began communicating upcoming events to Wayne via the refrigerator door, where the King of Snacks was likely to find a request to take Jenna to her Saturday dance class or a reminder of Rick's Thursday night pack meeting—along with a stern admonition to stay out of the cold cuts. And as often as not, Wayne became the one who took Jenna to the dance studio and Rick to Cub Scouts! Gleefully, I branched out.

"I have an early morning interview on Wednesday. Could you put the kids on the bus that morning? And leave the leftover ham alone—it's for a casserole tomorrow night!" Sure enough, I was freed to leave the house at 7:00 A.M. on Wednesday to make my interview date. "Parent/teacher conferences are Tuesday and Wednesday. Which one can you do? And stay out of the ice cream—I'm saving it for dessert." I would come across him making an entry in his pocket calendar of a conference with Rick's teacher on Tuesday morning. It all seemed manageable again, and all it took was a little written communication.

My wise friend Rosemary, who accurately describes herself as "almost too supporting and nurturing," had a little trouble getting over this management hurdle, too, although she and her executive husband Al have a long history of talking things out. When, after fourteen years of marriage, they welcomed their son Ryan into their lives, Rosemary realized she had gotten into the habit of doing too much herself and had stopped communicating her needs to Al as well as she used to. "I'll get to a point where I'll say, 'It's not fair. I'm doing more than my fair share here,' and Al will say, 'Okay. What do you need?' I'll tell him, and we'll work something out. But I can't stop resenting the fact that I have to ask. I want him to *know*, but how could he? He can't understand what's involved in the baby's schedule, all the planning and thinking ahead that has to be done over every little thing, like just packing a diaper bag, because he's never had to do it for an extended period of time. So unless I tell him, it doesn't occur to him."

Like listmaking, advance planning is an effective way to make the best possible use of limited time, as well as to get other members of the family to share in domestic tasks. Asking a teenager who's in the middle of a conversation with her boyfriend on the telephone to run down to the store for a loaf of bread is likely to be more trouble than it's worth in light of her inevitable protests and sulking. But if she's told on her way out the door to school that morning to pick up bread on her way home, warfare will probably be averted, and one stop will be eliminated from Mom's errand list.

Even daunting scheduling tasks, like finding a clear week for a family vacation, can be accomplished with advance planning. I have always resisted the idea of planned vacations, believing that spontaneity was at least half the fun. In the six years before we became parents, Wayne and I enjoyed several spur-of-the-moment trips. "Let's throw a few things into a suitcase and spend a long weekend in Bermuda," we said once and proceeded to suit actions to words. Or, "I can't wait until we have kids so we can take them to Disney World," Wayne confided another time, and two days later, we were on a plane headed south, and we had more fun than any two kids at that wonderful park. It was during such a trip to Florida, in fact, that I discovered I was pregnant with Ricky; and once he arrived, it seemed that all hope for spontaneous travel had been eliminated.

Though we day-tripped and made occasional sojourns to Boston or the seashore for an overnight stay, it was eight years before we actually took a bona-fide vacation again. Even then, it was almost forced upon us. Wayne had four weeks' vacation time each year, but at least two of those weeks were consumed caring for the kids during school vacations while I continued to work, since I had only two weeks' vacation from my job. We'd think about taking a trip, then decide we ought to stay home and paint the house, or something equally glamorous, instead. I figured that even if we planned a vacation, one of the kids would be sick or something. Then, about three years ago, when Ricky was six and Jenna was five, they saw Walt Disney World on television. "When can we go there?" Ricky demanded.

"You're too young to enjoy it fully yet," one of us responded vaguely. "When you're nine and Jenna's eight, we'll go." Intended as a diplomatic put-off, the remark instead triggered a relentless three-year countdown on the part of our offspring, who kept us posted on the time remaining to blast-off at regular intervals. At her sixth birthday, Jenna announced, "Two more years to Disney World!" and when Ricky did the same thing at his eighth, we resigned ourselves to the inevitable. A promise was a promise, however hastily made.

Still believing that any trip that had to be planned a year in advance (as a trip to Disney World must be, due to incredibly large numbers of advance bookings) could never live up to all that anticipation, I attempted to cool the kids' ardor with such remarks as, "You know, Disney World is very expensive. If we're going to spend a week there in the fall, we won't be able to afford any special trips this summer."

"Okay," they agreed promptly, and I trudged off to call the travel agent, who booked us for November. Gloomily, I anticipated all the things that would surely go wrong between now and November to thwart this vacation. In November one or both kids would surely be down with the flu. Wayne would be assigned to a thirty-day wiretap at the end of October. I wouldn't be able to find anyone to feed the cats. The School Board would object to our taking the kids out of class. But the first of November arrived *sans* germs or wiretap; the kids' teachers wished them *bon voyage*; and a family friend moved in to take care of the cats. It became clear that WE WERE GOING, but I remained unexcited. I was sick of hearing about the trip, planning the trip, talking about the damned trip. How could anything so unspontaneous be any fun?

It wasn't fun, as it turned out. It was *fantastic*. Our accommodations were glorious, the weather perfect, the crowds nonexistent—and all because of advanced planning. We sunned, swam, tramped our feet into numbness at Disney World and Epcot, rented a boat, a car, a golf cart, fed the peacocks that roamed freely outside our villa door, ate, drank, and were extremely merry for six wonderful days none of us will ever forget. To my delight, there were enough surprises to provide all the spontaneity even I could wish for: the splendor of the performing whales at Sea World; the forgotten delight of leaving cold and gray behind to re-enter summer magically; the pine cones of incredible size and perfection we collected for Grandma Polly's Christmas arrangements; the joy of teaching my beautiful daughter to dive—a skill I had almost forgotten I possessed; the laughter we shared when Ricky, solicitous after a long day in the sun, inquired of us gravely, "Would you care for some liquor?" We had planned the framework, not the actuality, and so had simply created a space in which anything might, and did, happen. It was one of my nicest lessons in time management.

Advance planning over even the short term can have similarly pleasant outcomes. That is, by keeping ahead of the game through planning, we can create windows of opportunity for spontaneous pleasures. For example, I don't let the income-tax return go until the last minute because I know our New England weather can turn from winter to summer in the blink of an eye in April, and if it does, I'll want to take off for a picnic at the beach instead of toiling over a hot calculator. If possible, I don't schedule any business appointments on Wednesdays, because my mother and I may take it into our heads to hop on the bus to New York and see a Broadway matinée. We don't do it every Wednesday, obviously, but the possibility is always dangling there pleasantly.

Actually, I can't ever recall that I regretted getting something done ahead of time. More often than not, in fact, doing so has saved my sanity, my professional reputation, my relationship with my husband and kids, or all three. A writer's life is governed by deadlines, and a writer who doesn't meet them 99.9 percent of the time may as well hang it up. As my kids are learning from their homework assignments, which aren't much fun to do at 8:00 P.M. Sunday when they'd rather be watching "Murder, She Wrote" with me, it's nearly impossible to perform at peak effectiveness with one fearful eye on the clock. Besides, life has a way of complicating already tight schedules. If you're late for a meeting, you'll be sure to have a flat tire or be caught in heavy traffic on the way. If you haven't allowed time to stop at the store for a spare pair of stockings, you'll certainly snag the ones you're wearing on the way to an important interview. Similarly, if you haven't finished your work ahead of schedule, something fun that you've always wanted to do will present itself the night before the job is due.

Nothing turns my brain to cement faster than having a client say, "Quick! Think of something madly creative!" When that happens, I'm lucky to be able to come up with my name, let alone a catchy slogan, title, or approach to promoting a product. So, whenever possible, I accept assignments with enough lead time to allow a relatively leisurely thought process, and when the bulb of inspiration lights, I waste no time transferring thoughts to paper well in advance of the project's due-date. That way, if I wake up the next morning and find my idea not so much whimsical as it is cloying, I have a chance to avoid embarrassing myself and to make some revisions. If, on rereading, I feel as satisfied with the copy as I did when I first wrote it, well and good. I can go buy the latest John D. MacDonald book and enjoy it with a clear conscience, and if Wayne calls from work to suggest a family night out, I can say, "Great, let's do it," instead of groaning about an uncompleted assignment. For me, keeping up with things is another way of keeping my options open.

Another way of looking at time management is priority setting. By taking care of predictable, low-priority tasks on a scheduled basis, I can take advantage of unpredictable, high-priority opportunities. By getting the housework and laundry out of the way on Friday, I can be open to drop-in guests, last-minute invitations, and spontaneous family activities that would otherwise be hectic. It's like having money in the bank for a rainy day, only in this case, I'm saving time for a sunny day.

On the job, time management is often the determinant between mediocre and superior performance. When I was employed in the sales promotion unit of a corporate advertising department, I was just one of several equally talented copywriters; but because I consistently turned the work out on time as well, my performance ratings were always higher than the others'. Nothing earns higher marks with a harrassed supervisor, who apologetically asks if by any chance an assignment might be completed ahead of the original deadline, than hearing a cheerful, "Here you go! I finished it up yesterday,"—that is, if the surprise doesn't kill him. It's a message I keep trying to get across to the kids, who see no reason—ever—for doing anything that isn't fun one minute before they absolutely HAVE TO.

I have also attempted to point out to them, now and again, how much time they consume talking about how much they have to do when they could be doing it and getting on with more enjoyable things. It's an easy trap to fall into, and if you don't get over the tendency as a kid, it can easily become a self-fulfilling prophecy. "I have soooo much to do!" is the trademark opening gambit of a woman I know, though mercifully, I see her only infrequently. She is a high-school counselor, a job which affords her a great deal more vacation time than most other working mothers, yet her life, to hear her tell it, is in perpetual chaos. Lounging comfortably in whatever seat presents itself, she will hold forth *ad nauseam* about how unmanageable it all is, apparently oblivious of the fact that three quarters of the other women present manage equally demanding schedules very handily. "There's no way I can possibly get it all done," she announces with great satisfaction, and because she spends much more time talking about it than doing it, she's absolutely right.

As any working mother will attest, there are times when no amount of advance planning and conscientious preparation can head off a hectic spell. Kids get sick, cars and appliances break down, deadlines change, and all those well-laid plans go right down the well-known bathroom appurtenance. But even then, there are ways to manage the seemingly unmanageable.

"When things get really out of hand," says Sarah, a tax attorney and the mother of three boisterous children, "I focus on the next two things I absolutely must do, no more. Viewed at 7:00 A.M., a hectic day can defeat you right then unless you break it into more manageable chunks. Think of it as looking down 300 miles of highway and envisioning all the hazards you might encounter. You'd never get out of the driveway. But if you concentrate on the first two blocks, and then the next two, and so on, you'll complete the journey successfully."

By consciously developing tunnel vision on over-crowded days, Sarah has repeatedly accomplished more than she ever thought possible in a fifteen-hour period and with far less emotional upheaval. "The last such day I remember was Babs' christening. Lew and I had decided to make a real event out of it, inviting all the cousins, old friends and neighbors we hadn't seen for a while, and my new boss and his wife. Our budget was ruined for months, but we even went so far as to hire a caterer to prepare some fancy goodies, though to keep costs down, I planned to heat and pass things around myself. Then, the night before the christening, Lew broke his foot." A sympathetic neighbor watched the children until Sarah and Lew returned from the hospital, where the bone had been set and Lew's foot and ankle encased in plaster. Midnight found them huddled over cocoa wondering how on earth they would cope. What had promised to be a festive day now loomed like a specter. Sarah especially dreaded the possibility of things not going well since she had invited her new boss and his wife to the event. "Partly, I wanted to show off my family, but mostly, I wanted to demonstrate to them how well I was managing to combine my career and my home life. My ego was really on the line," she confided.

By dawn's early light, Sarah nursed baby Babs and ruthlessly slashed her plans to the bone, simplifying the menu to exclude hot hors d'oeuvres and anything else that required a lot of attention. Having telephoned the caterer with the bad news, she decided what two things had to be accomplished next to avert total disaster: grooming herself and the kids. "I figured that if we all looked as if things were under control, we'd believe it, so I spent a precious hour doing my hair and makeup and shepherding John and Justin into their new suits while Babs napped. Lew, meanwhile, drew up a sketch of how the bar should be laid out to facilitate self-service, and the boys carried it out. He knew the boys were dying to get into the act, so he let them help. They probably learned more about etiquette and social decorum that afternoon than they will for the rest of their lives."

The next two things were getting to the church on time and getting Lew safely through the service. The two things after that were beating the guests home and nursing Babs so she wouldn't be hungry during the party. The next two things were greeting the guests and making sure her boss and his wife had someone to talk with, and so on throughout the afternoon. Then came the curve ball. "Over a last glass of sherry, Mr. Farnsworth complimented me elaborately on handling the party so successfully in spite of Lew's accident, especially, he said, when he knew I had an important client meeting scheduled first thing in the morning. I almost bit through my glass. I had completely forgotten the meeting, for which I had planned to prepare the previous evening when I was at the hospital with Lew." Though she felt like screaming, Sarah smilingly ushered the Farnsworths to the door while concentrating on the *next* two things she had to do.

"It all turned out all right. Everybody went home; the kids and I got the worst of the clutter cleared up. I fed Babs and went over the client's tax return in the upstairs bedroom. Lew went to bed with a brandy and some aspirin, inviting the boys to watch a TV movie with him so I could continue working. By ten o'clock, everyone was asleep, and a terribly hectic day was behind us."

It had been a memorable day for more than one reason, but not nearly as bad as it would have been if Sarah had not taken it one step—make that two steps—at a time.

4

REDEFINITIONS

Coping successfully with the domestic double standard, and working toward its elimination, is as much a matter of attitude as it is one of action—and the attitudes of contemporary women and their families have changed considerably over the past two decades.

By taking a fresh look at what they really want from their lives, today's women have redefined "success" in positive, but more realistic, terms. In much the same way, they have given new meaning to "having it all" by recognizing the need for more balance in their lives.

Having proven to themselves and to the world that they can do it all, women are making new choices about how best to meet their real needs. They are, in short, redefining "success" in personal, rather than societal, terms, and the domestic double standard figures prominently in this redefinition.

REDEFINING SUCCESS

"HOW DID YOU DO IT all those years?" a new mother of my acquaintance asked me recently, referring to my eight years of full-time work while simultaneously bearing and rearing two small children and completing a college degree. "I really have to give you credit!" While I have no doubt that her admiration was genuine, I sensed a slight undertone of "What are you, a masochist?" in her query, now that she is acquainted with the difficulties of juggling career and motherhood. It's tough, very tough, she now knows, so her question was not so much, "How did you do it?" as, "*Why* did you do it?"

Why, indeed? At this moment, I can't honestly cite a specific reason. Apparently my Superwoman phase was just another lengthy stage in the struggle toward what Betty Friedan termed "personhood." Knowing what I do now, I would not voluntarily repeat the experience, nor would I encourage others to follow in my steps. Once I discovered that having it all meant doing it all, the game lost much of its appeal, and I am far from being alone in that discovery.

As men have known practically forever, having a

career can be enormously exciting. It is thrilling when the ideas pop, the adrenalin flows, and the money rolls in. But the most stimulating occupation in the world can pall after ten or fifteen years, and if often does, leaving us to inquire of our middle-aged reflections in the mirror, "So, what do you want to be when you grow up?"

Perhaps it is a sign of these hectic times that we are tackling the mid-life crisis rather earlier than age forty these days, confronting our nagging doubts about the wisdom of earlier choices and our suppressed dissatisfactions somewhere around our mid-thirties. "Just avoiding the rush," we assure each other coyly. But if the first such period of internal probing occurs at age thirty-five, after only a decade or so on a chosen course, can we not expect another crisis at, say, age fifty? Well, why not? What after all is the point of having the options created, for women and men both, by the women's movement, if we never pause to consider and choose from among them? Presumably, the changes we make in our lives as a result will be for the better, more accurately reflecting new needs and priorities that have crept stealthily into our awareness in the interval since our last appraisal. I say, go for it at least every ten years!

When I was 18, I was not surprised that I did not know what I wanted to do with the rest of my life, as my high school guidance counselor seemed to expect. I was surprised, though, that at the age of thirty-five, I still didn't know—surprised, but not dismayed. I knew what I wanted to do for the next five years, and I was content with that knowledge. Now, in fact, I find it delightful to contemplate my freedom to make future choices at intervals, opting to explore a new project here, a new goal there. As *women* have known forever, options are what liberation is all about, and unless I'm mistaken, men are finally beginning to understand what's in it for them.

"If I were you, Tina, I wouldn't work at all," says her husband Bill—a wistful and revealing statement. However, if Tina's new career as a toy manufacturer's sales representative turns out to be as enjoyable and lucrative as it might, Bill may discover a greater number of options in his own life.

"If you can make as much money as I do," Michele's husband Rudy tells her, "I'll trade places with you." Well, perhaps she can, and perhaps he will.

"I worked for the first twenty years," says Millie's husband Carl. "It's your turn." Though spoken mostly in jest, his words have the ring of wishful thinking.

Bill, Rudy, and Carl represent the growing number of husbands who are realizing that they, too, can make new choices about the way they want to spend their lives instead of locking themselves into one inflexible pattern for the duration. In recent years, many have experimented with the reversal of traditional men's and women's roles, with him assuming primary responsibility for children and the household and her earning the family's income.

Cynthia, an attractive and energetic fifty-year-old, who after thirty years with a Connecticut insurance company is its highest ranking female officer, tells about her experiences with role reversal. "About four years ago, my husband got very discouraged with his job. He had been teaching for about eighteen years, and I really think he burned out. Every day it was a chore for him to get up and go to work. I finally said to him, 'Why are you putting yourself through this? You really don't have to. We give Uncle Sam half our salary anyway, so why are you doing this to yourself?' So he decided that he would quit and that he would stay home, believe it or not, and take care of the house. So John and I have done kind of a complete role reversal.

"John is mainly responsible for laundry and shopping and errands, which is just wonderful, because I don't have to spend Saturday now running around to eight different places to do eight different things. I even got clever enough to say to my children, when they didn't have clean clothes, 'I don't do laundry anymore. Your father does the laundry, and if you can't get him to listen, you're going to have to do it yourself.' That was my first big liberated step, and I thought that was marvelous! Our new arrangement has worked very well for us. I don't know that either of us was certain that it would work when we entered into it, but it has. John still stays at home, and he doesn't mind doing all the things that he is supposed to do during the week. In fact, he enjoys a lot of it. He doesn't do everything that a woman would do if she stayed at home, and he probably never will. For instance, I still cook. I have a hard time sitting and drinking my glass of wine while my husband is puttering around the kitchen. So he doesn't do the cooking, and he doesn't change the closets over from season to season or anything like that, but I really don't mind. Generally, we feel that we've settled into what are very comfortable roles for us right now. We accept the fact that we were probably about a decade before our time in terms of my going back to work and all of what that meant, and then the role reversal thing. We also know ourselves well enough to know that if we had it to do over again, we'd probably do the same thing."

As positive as the potential of role reversal is, the motives behind it are critical. For example, it is possible that a man may simply be yearning to free himself from the corporate rat race so strongly that he fantasizes about the joys of domestic life, then finds the reality most unsatisfactory. Running from a negative situation into an unknown alternative can turn an already bad scene into a disaster, as more than one couple has discovered.

Peter and Candace met and married while both were in law school in the early 1970s. Though they graduated simultaneously, only Peter went on to join a small but growing firm of legal consultants specializing in real estate, while Candace remained at home to raise a son and, three years later, a daughter. After eight years, Peter dared his wife, who for years had complained about feeling stifled and isolated, to trade places with him. "After all those years, during which I habitually discussed every detail of my work with Candace on a daily basis, I felt certain she knew as much about real estate law as I did. She had kept up with her professional reading, and even more important, she was dying to get out there and knock 'em dead. What I wanted to do was to drop out altogether, take over everything she had been doing at home while she took over as a breadwinner. One night, we looked at each other and said, 'Why not?'"

The "why not," it turned out, was both Peter and Candace's totally unrealistic visions of each other's roles. As agreed, Peter stayed at home in their newly acquired house in rural New Hampshire, caring for the children and doing all of the cooking and cleaning, while Candace began work with a local land developer. Their first mistake was believing that either of them was equipped to perform their new jobs as well as the other had. Though obviously a bright and capable woman, Candace lacked Peter's eight years of practical experience in the field and did not, as a result, command nearly the salary he had. And when she returned home at night, she found ample evidence of Peter's inexperience as a householder. The house was always a mess, the dinner either burned or forgotten, the children running wild. She would rush about, exasperated, attempting to set things right while Peter groused about the inadequacy of their reduced household budget and his resentment of the same domestic double standard about which Candace had so recently complained. As the months went on, the two adopted martyred attitudes, fending off attacks on their abilities by pointing out to each other the incredible difficulties of role reversal.

Eventually, they stopped squabbling and sat down to reassess their options. Now that neither of them any longer had a fantasy vision of the other's work, they were able to redefine their priorities in ways consistent with the realities of their situation. Together, they have set up a small practice not far from their home and share both professional and domestic responsibilities on alternating shifts. Their relationship has been restablized on an equal footing, combining the best of their professional and domestic skills in accordance with the needs and wishes of both. Future experiments, they agree, will be less drastic and better planned.

* * *

Of course there are men who seem devoted to their chosen careers and accepting of the limitations these impose on other aspects of their lives. I used to think, in fact, that Wayne was one of them. So it came as quite a surprise when he remarked about two years ago, on his fortieth birthday, that he had exactly nine years and eight months to put in before he could retire from government service. Why, exactly, was he counting? Had the job from which he'd been virtually inseparable for those many years finally lost its appeal? To some extent, yes, he responded with alarming promptness. Twelve years battling the bad guys, bureaucrats, and an incomprehensible judicial system was one thing, but the prospect of another 10 years in the same trenches excited him very little. Cautiously, I inquired further.

The trade-offs Wayne had so willingly accepted at age twenty-eight to embark upon a career in law enforcement were not nearly as palatable at mid-life, he explained. The long hours, the lengthy commuting, the frequent travel were still manageable, but he was far more aware of their impact on his life and less convinced that his limited ability to participate in other activities was worth the attractive pension he would gain ten years hence. He had even gone so far as to inquire about the financial penalties for early retirement, which would free him a few years sooner to pursue other interests. By now, he had my complete attention. "What other interests?" I asked, attempting to adjust to this surprising revelation while feeling our financial bedrock shift ominously beneath me.

Well, he confided in a rush, he had always enjoyed woodworking. His father had been an accomplished carpenter, and Wayne had picked up more than even he had realized as a kid. He was forever helping this friend or that with major repairs and additions to their houses, and he had constructed built-in bookcases in our house and a sturdy storage shed in the yard. It was a skill he really wanted to develop further, he said, and maybe even build a house one day. Or two.

I felt dazed. At that time, I too was engaged in redefining my career, but then, it seemed as though I had been doing that throughout our married life. Yet whereas my changing jobs constituted no big deal in our family, Wayne's contemplation of doing so was quite another matter. It had never occurred to me that he would pursue any other course but law enforcement for another ten years, then return to pharmacy, his field of education, but on a more leisurely basis that would give him more free time to sail his boat, which had been languishing beside the garage for years. Building houses represented quite a departure from this plan; but on further thought, why should Wayne be any more restricted in his life options than I? Was the man not entitled to the same freedom of choice I enjoyed?

Over the next few weeks, we talked about the future a lot, figuring out how we might accumulate sufficient funds to purchase an attractive building lot not too far from our home on which Wayne would eventually raise a single-family house. The sale of the first house would provide financing for a second, and so on. It was fun to talk about it. Wayne was more enthusiastic than I'd seen him in years as we weighed the relative merits of building a house from scratch or renovating an existing structure, of buying beach property or a suburban tract. He whistled and hummed. The sketch pad I hadn't seen him use in a dog's age reappeared. Brochures describing various carpentry workshops began arriving in the mail. The following August, Wayne enrolled in one and trekked off to the woods of Massachusetts for a week to be instructed in the fine art of structural renovation. My husband, the house-builder, I wondered. Was this a whim?

Nearly two years later, I can assure you that it was not. A savings plan is in effect which will amass the funds necessary to purchase a building lot within five years. A laboriously constructed cardboard replica of our house resides on the desk in the master bedroom, presaging the addition Wayne will tackle next spring by way of rehearsal for the main event. Whether or not he will wait until age fifty to retire from government service remains undecided, but for the moment, the knowledge that we *both* have options has done wonders. We hug more. We talk more. It's nice.

No doubt, Wayne's original twenty-two-year commitment to the Drug Enforcement Administration delayed his realization of the choices that remained his to make, for my inquiries among friends and colleagues have revealed that a whole lot more redefining of "success" is going on out there than I ever suspected—by men, by women, and better yet, by men and women together. The freedom to do so is largely attributable to the increased earning power of women to whom new employment opportunities have been opened, fattening the family coffers and widening the spectrum of choices available to both partners.

Rosemary and Al, our friends who waited fourteen years before having a baby in order to make significant progress toward their goal of financial independence, have found that their new son Ryan has prompted some important changes in their thinking. "Our priorities have changed, in that leisure time has become extremely important, and material goals—that is, 'things'—are not as important," Rosemary explains. "We still want to have accumulated some assets by a certain point, say, five years from now, but wanting 'things' has changed for us. We've found that buying things doesn't really make you happy, so I think we've done some growing in that area. When I was twenty, I thought it would be really wonderful if I could have a huge mansion one day with twelve rooms of furniture. Now, what I'd like is time to spend with my son and my husband, which was the idea behind my consulting business. There's more leisure time.

My goal is to work hard now so we can have more time later—it's future-oriented. We're paying a price now so we can reach a goal later on. If anything, we lower our standard of living as time goes on, rather than raise it. We now make more than five times what we did when we were first married, but the money means something different now—more flexibility, not buying a more expensive house. Most of our friends at our income level have the Jacuzzis and the saunas, the swimming pool and the country club. We just try to maintain an upper middle-class standard of living, because our goal is not just to keep accumulating more things but to gain more time together. What would sadden me the most would be if someday we looked back and said, 'You know, we never took the time we should have with our son,' or 'We never had the time together we wanted.' I figure by the time Ryan is five, both Al and I will have incredible amounts of time to spend with him."

A small, relatively new trend would seem to indicate that some women are redefining success as the freedom to stop working outside the home, even when they do not have children for whom to care. In a March 1985 *Washington Post* article, Stephanie Mansfield reported on the "Women's Stay-Home Syndrome" in which a growing number of professional women who have spent the last decade making all the right career moves are giving up their high-paying jobs and prestigious titles to stay home and take advantage of other life options open to them. Mansfield quotes Sally Schmidt, a thirty-two-year-old New York City attorney who recently left the work force. "Women got into the men's schools and braved the work world. What they found is that men have only one choice. For women—this may sound sort of anti-feminist—but we're capable of being successful in other ways." Schmidt was a member of the second class at Yale to admit women, and she received a law degree from Vanderbilt. After five years as an associate with a Manhattan law firm, she quit, defying the current women's trend of careerism.

Mansfield also quotes Rhoda Frindell Green, a career counselor and psychologist based in New York, who believes that the drop-out syndrome among professional women is significant. "Society's pressures for women to achieve are super-high now. It's been building since the late 1960s. In fact, the pressure is similar to the pressure society put on women in the 1950s to marry and have children." This is an unwelcome backlash of the women's movement that many of us have experienced. Years ago, our husbands were embarrassed if we worked outside the home. Now they, and we, are usually embarrassed if we don't.

Women are leaving the careers they worked so hard to achieve for a number of reasons, not the least of which is their growing awareness that they "sold out" to that kind of societal pressure instead of choosing to work for positive, personal reasons. Having proven to themselves and to the world that they can do it all, they are taking a breather to get back in touch with their real needs and priorities and to make new choices about how best to meet them. They are, in short, redefining "success" in personal, rather than traditional career, terms, and the domestic double standard figures prominently in this redefinition.

Prior to the birth of her first child in 1980, Deanne was feeling guilty about not having achieved the kind of success for which she had always felt destined. "Here I was, thirty-one years old, married, and the tape that played in my head said, 'You don't have a child yet. You're supposed to have a child by now. You don't have your Ph.D., and you're supposed to have your Ph.D. by now. You were the whiz kid at age twenty-one when you were on a fellowship, but it's ten years later, Deanne.' There were a lot of other things going on in my head, and finally, I admitted to myself that I didn't want an academic life on a college campus teaching eighteen-year-olds who were wet behind the ears. Something didn't feel right in all of this.

"What happened, somewhere in the mid-1970s, was my getting involved on a grass-roots basis with the women's movement, study groups in which a lot of women were coming together and saying, 'Something doesn't feel right,' and not being sure what that something was. Very quickly, because I'm not good at staying quiet for long periods of time, I realized that there were people here to organize, people who were saying the same things I was but who weren't ready to take some sort of leadership position. I decided, along with some other women, that I was, and we began to organize similar groups in other areas. And all of a sudden, strange things started to happen." Deanne's talent for organizing groups of women and helping them to clarify their life objectives was immediately apparent to everyone with whom she came in contact, and her volunteer activism quickly led into paid work opportunities. A consciousness-raising seminar at the local Jewish community center led to a request from the Town of West Hartford, Connecticut, to conduct a course on women's issues for its municipal employees, to invitations from radio stations to discuss women's issues on the air, to speaking engagements all over the state, and then to an offer to teach in a community college's continuing education program. Response to the course was so positive that Deanne was soon invited to develop other courses for the college's regular undergraduate curriculum. "But still," she says, "nothing had jelled. This was not my work, it was my hobby. My work was the Ph.D. that I wasn't doing. But at a 1978 trainers' workshop, I was talking about what I loved to do versus this albatross around my neck, the Ph.D., and somebody said to me, 'You know what's wrong? Your work is your hobby, and your hobby is your work. You should think of your Ph.D. as your hobby, because you only do your hobby when you feel like it. Your work is your mission in life. You have made a mission out of human-resources development, and you've done it really well, but you haven't claimed it.' My God, it was better than sex! In three sentences, he had solved the whole problem."

At another workshop some six months later, Deanne was advised to start her own business and given an overnight assignment to create a plan on how she would launch it. "I said, okay, I'll develop a seven-year plan, because that's how long it would take, and the workshop leader said, 'It's a seven-month plan. Don't give me this seven years crap.' I stayed up the whole night, mostly worrying about how I could possibly do this in seven months, and all of a sudden it dawned on me that I was making mountains out of molehills. All I needed to do was print stationery, print cards, identify my product and my market area, and tell the people I was already servicing that I was now doing this as a business. So I came back with a plan for developing the business in seven *weeks*!"

Suiting actions to words, Deanne followed through. "Basically, I just started printing my course materials on letterhead paper instead of plain white paper and telling clients that this was no longer Deanne, this nice fly-by-night person, but Deanne in business for herself, and most of my clients came through word-of-mouth advertising, which was wonderful."

Having discarded her long-held notion that her life work would consist of acquiring a Ph.D. and settling into university teaching, Deanne had taken the first significant step toward redefining success for herself, but it was years before she put it all together, she says. What she had defined as her "work" was developing nicely, but she remained uncertain about how a baby would fit into her life and still cherished her involvement as a community activist, when time permitted. Following the birth of her son Douglas in 1980, she developed a great and abiding respect for work within the home—a feeling that deepened when second son Elliot arrived in 1983. "Aside from the fact that I think my sons are gorgeous and wonderful and all that nice parental sort of stuff, they really are terrific little people. I like the idea of having time with them at home and seeing some of my values coming through, the things I believe in and work on in the world with clients. So what's changed is that I now see more than one aspect of my work in the world. I like the image that everybody has a life work. I used to think that I had only one, and it was just a question of figuring out what it was. I thought it would be my product for which I got paid. First, I thought it would be teaching religion, and then I thought it would be personal and professional development facilitation. Now, one piece is definitely that. I help provide people with the tools to empower themselves. But a second piece is doing exactly the same thing in my family. It became very clear to me that that was what raising children was about, helping to empower little ones to become real human beings."

The third piece of her life work, Deanne now knows, is community work. "I had always been an active volunteer, and I thought of it as important, but I didn't necessarily think of it as part of my work. I thought that nice people volunteer and help those less fortunate, but I didn't see it as social change work. Now, I do. Along with others, I've created an alternative Jewish community in this area, mainly because we weren't satisfied with what was here, and we've had a real impact on this community, creating something viable for lots of people. So now my work is about one-third, one-third, one-third split."

Each of the pieces is very important to Deanne, she says, on the level of values, and on a psychological level in terms of who she is in the world, and she cannot imagine any one of them ever falling away. "Obviously, kids grow up, but I expect to be involved in some aspect of family development for a significant period. I really want independent, autonomous children who have room to develop their own values, like the people I want to see out in the world, and I don't think that happens by saying, 'Bye, kids. I'll see you when you're eighteen.' Also, I need to have control over my life, and for me, the best way to do that is to be the chief." Managing her own consulting business has given Deanne that control, allowing her to accommodate the other aspects of her work.

"I really do feel successful right now, because I've made the decision about how to put together the three pieces in the formula. Family life is critically important to me, along with work in the outside world and community activism. Those are my values, and I want what I do in this life to represent my values. They aren't values if you don't act on them! Success, to me, is having the freedom to define all the pieces of myself, the right to do it, and the ability to make them happen."

I could not agree more, but I would go a step further. As we continue to struggle with the task of juggling multiple and equally demanding roles, success means the freedom and ability to *re*define the pieces of ourselves according to needs and priorities that inevitably change with the passage of time; and as we make progress in our struggle to ameliorate the domestic double standard that persists, at this moment, in imposing limits on our lives, I am convinced that we will have increasing opportunities for such personal redefinition.

Men, too, will benefit from these opportunities, as Rosemary is quick to point out, and I'll let her have the last word here. Today, she says, men still tend to focus on the workplace as the arena in which they will have "success," while women are busy organizing additional opportunities for successful experiences—for themselves and for their male partners. "I think women have more perspective," she reflects. "Maybe we've been raised to have these kinds of skills, so we keep building these really strong women. The thing is, we've got to start building really strong men. I think men focus so much on their careers that they get one-sided. It's too bad for them, because they don't develop that circle of friends and those loving relationships with their sons and daughters. We've got to stress to our sons—and of course, our daughters will be listening, too—that success is not only in a career. There's got to be a balance between career and family.

"It's not so important that you make it up the corporate ladder. What's important is getting what *you* want in life, not that other people see you as their kind of success. People who give their lives to one thing only are usually not that happy, although there are people who are so very talented at their work that they genuinely prefer to give it all their time and energy. But the average man needs to diversify, just like a woman. Don't give it all to a career, and don't give it all to the kids. Don't give it all to your spouse or to yourself, either. Try to balance all four together, if you can."

Amen.

Whether a woman decides to have it all at once or one step at a time is an individual decision, and the extent to which she eliminates the domestic double standard in her household is largely dependent on her individual actions. This, perhaps, is how it should be during the second stage of the women's movement.

HAVING IT ALL (REVISITED)

TEN YEARS AGO LETITIA BALDRIDGE, probably best known as social secretary to the White House during the Kennedy administration, wrote a book called *Juggling: The Art of Balancing Marriage, Motherhood, and Career.* Explaining her reasons for doing so, she cited an encounter with a potential client for her public relations company, the chairman of the board for one of the largest corporations in the country. "He gave me a half-hour appointment to listen to my carefully prepared, well-articulated public relations proposal for his company. At the end, his first words were, 'Tish, why isn't a nice girl like you home taking care of your husband and children?' It takes an entire book to answer him. I shudder to think how many more chairmen of the board there are just like him."

Quite a few, apparently, since a decade later we find ourselves still swimming upstream against a current of out-of-date thinking—in greater numbers, perhaps, but not quite as far along in our journey as we had expected to be by now. The goal of equality, in the work place and in the home, is a lot farther off than we thought initially; and so, we are shifting gears, slowing the pace just a bit as we settle in for the long haul.

Despite what we were encouraged to believe years ago, Dr. Barbara Mackoff, author of *Leaving the Office Behind,* says that the only women who have it all are the ones in the perfume commercials—those impeccably groomed creatures who croon that they can bring home the bacon, fry it up in the pan, and never let him forget he's a man. But, she asked at a recent lecture, is that really what we want? She suggested that what we really mean today by "having it all" is having the freedom to choose from it all, to know that the options are there and to select those that mean the most to us as individual women.

There is no doubt that having it all is possible, but more and more often, women are asking themselves, at what price? And if the price is too high at a given moment for our limited time and energy resources, some judicious budgeting is in order. "Is having it all still worth it to you?" I asked friends and colleagues, and the answer was, "Yes, *but* . . ."

Yes, *but,* says Rosemary, "I think there should always be a mental and physical balance. It's a cliché, but you've got to find out what makes you happy." What counts, she adds, is that you don't become somebody who only does things for and through other people—or because others attempt to impose their preferences on you. "If someone is working because she thinks others believe she should be working, she just has to step back and say, 'Hey, this is *my* life, and who am I doing this for?' I don't like this judgmental crap, this 'I'm better than you are because I'm earning money.' The negative side of women who work full time and have kids, too, is a tendency to say, 'Hey, look, I'm Superwoman here, and what are *you* doing?' Sometimes, it does work out better to do it all simultaneously, but I would never look down on a woman who wasn't involved in both a career and children at the same time."

* * *

While the 1980s woman is just as committed to having it all as her 1960s sisters were, she is taking a more thoughtful, long-term view of her future, considering the merits of having it all sequentially instead of simultaneously in an orderly progression of work- and home-focused periods that allow her to concentrate the majority of her attention and energy in one or the other arena. In the early years of her career, she may find it more satisfying not to have to divide herself between job and home and so postpones having children until she has reached initial career goals. Then, knowing her career hiatus is only temporary, she is far more likely to enjoy her years as primary caretaker for her children, and the domestic double standard is less likely to impose a frustrating burden.

Rosemary is a member of this camp. "I like to keep my options open. I have lots of goals, but I no longer feel I have to reach them all by the age of 40. That's why it's fine to take the time now to give my son my priority. I can do it differently later. If I were going to advise somebody, I'd say try to work it out so you've got some time to enjoy your kids, because you can't live it again. With your career you can always say, 'Oh, hell, I blew it on that job,' and go out and get a different job. You only get one chance at a kid."

Though she has chosen to give her son a lot of intensive time right now, Rosemary fully intends at some point to pursue her career more aggressively, adjusting the amounts of time and energy she devotes to job and family as the years go by. "You can get it all," she says, "but you just don't get it all at once sometimes. I try to tell my friends who get frustrated, because there's just not enough time to do anything for themselves, 'There'll be plenty of time later—probably, more than you want. Enjoy what you've got now, because you're going to have time to do all those things you can't do now."

Patti, who at age twenty-six is making her three small children her top priority for the time being, is another who has decided to have it all sequentially. She reflects on whether she would do things differently—become established in a career and have her children later—knowing what she now knows. "There's a good possibility I'd do the same thing over. For one thing, the younger you are, the more patience you tend to have with the kids and the more physical stamina you have, and you need that. You have to be physically and mentally ready to cope. Also, as I get older I'm thinking on a more mature level. I have a better idea of what I want to do for a career. When you get out of high school, you might go for anything, but when you get older, your ideas are more clearly defined. Another benefit of doing it this way is that we are still going to be young when the kids are grown, and then we can have time for ourselves."

These women and others make a solid case for having it all sequentially, but an equal number believe it is not only desirable but necessary—for them—to combine career and motherhood simultaneously. I am a member of this camp, but in answer to the question, "Is having it all still worth it?" we, too, reply, "Yes, *but* . . ."

Yes, *but* it is essential that you be able to share the domestic burden, says Katherine, a teacher whose early years as a working mother were made considerably easier by her husband, a university professor. "We've always been able to manage our schedules so that I could work reasonably comfortably. If I'd married someone else, it would have been a lot tougher," she maintains. "Neil is very happy with his job, but his job has never come first. I'm spoiled, I really am. I don't do the garbage; I don't do the checking; I don't do the vacuuming; and I think he does more laundry than I do. Neil can't cook, but he's very good with frozen food, putting it in the microwave! His father never did anything around the house, so I don't know why he turned out the way he did." Whatever the reason, Katherine says she is well aware of the difference a supportive partner has made in her life. "If I hadn't been married to Neil, who can usually arrange his schedule around the family's needs if I can't, I might have looked for more work like tutoring, which is more flexible. But when a full-time teaching position came open and I told Neil I'd really like to get back full time, he worked his schedule out so he was around with our daughters when I wasn't."

Because of the support she receives from her husband, as well as from her two daughters, now fifteen and ten, Katherine has been able over the years to combine her teaching career and family responsibilities without undue stress. "I work because I enjoy it. If you asked me on a Friday afternoon at 3:30, I probably wouldn't tell you that, but I like to have something that's mine, not just be a shadow in Neil's life. I like my own identity. Also, it's important to me to know I can earn my own living. I like the idea that I can go out and buy two pairs of shoes and not feel the least bit guilty because I'm helping out financially. And I really couldn't stay at home. I don't know what I'd do! I could do volunteer work," she chuckles, "but in one of the school systems I taught in, I felt as if I was volunteering myself anyway! We all did, for what we got paid."

Now that her children are growing up, Katherine says things are getting even easier to manage. "We'll talk it over and decide who's going to cook, and I'll come home and find chicken teriyaki all ready to eat. My older daughter is a great cook—and whoever cooks doesn't do the dishes, which is one reason why she likes it. Everybody helps, so its not as hard now, and the kids think it's kind of nice that I work. They both know that what *I* do is going to help them do what *they* want to do, like go to college, because I tell them!"

Not every woman is as fortunate in her family's attitude toward sharing household work, of course. In most homes, in fact, there is still an enormous gap between husbands' and children's good intentions of sharing the domestic burden and what actually transpires, but strong indications of progress in overcoming the domestic double standard are evident even so.

Deanne, for example, is lavish in praising her husband's willing attitude, but she admits there is room for improvement. "I have to give credit where credit is due. I think Ted is unusually cooperative when it comes to the kids. He has been far more involved and supportive than I expected, first of all, and also far more so than any other father I know. However, the difference is in who does the figuring out and planning. This morning was a perfect example. We got back from New York at two o'clock this morning, and I said to him, 'I need you to take the kids to school and day-care today,' and he said, 'Okay, great.' Normally, when I say that, he does it all. He gets the boys up and gets them washed, and he feeds them and packs their bags and takes them out the door. But he drove last night, and he was exhausted, so I decided today that I'd get up and nurse the baby and get lunches made. Ted did breakfast for the baby. He got them washed, and I got their clothes together. All that was pretty fair teamwork, but they got out to the front door, and it didn't occur to Ted, with all his involvement, that Douglas hadn't brushed his teeth. And that is to me *the* example of what you're talking about. I mean, men know that children have teeth, and it's not like it's the first time that Douglas's teeth have had to be brushed. You'd think that it wouldn't have to be me, who was not supposed to be on duty this morning, who had to remember that."

Sometimes, Deanne suggests, the best way to help your partner understand the full implications of the domestic double standard is not to help him at all, which is often more difficult than it sounds. "I was going to a five-day national convention, leaving Ted responsible for getting the kids to and from school and child care and being with them at night and during the weekend I would be gone. Just before I left here, Ted said, 'We have a problem. I have to be in Philadelphia Monday morning.' And I said, 'No, we don't have a problem. *You* have a problem, because you've got to figure out how to provide for the kids from Sunday night to Monday night. You've known for six months that I'm going. So either tell the vice president you're not going, or figure out an answer."

She really had to grit her teeth, Deanne says, because her instinct was to come up with the right answer—a faster and better answer than Ted would. With an effort of will, however, she declined to deal with the situation, and predictably, Ted solved the problem. "He got his brother to come, and he made arrangements with the nursery school and with the child-care person for some coverage. When I came back at midnight Monday, the kids were safely in a place with a responsible adult. I really had to clamp down hard on myself, though I'm sure I spent some time wondering if the kids would be alive when I got off that plane. But I did turn off worrying about whether or not their teeth were brushed. I knew they wouldn't be, but you've got to pick your fights!"

Having it all, to Deanne, is finding a way to combine motherhood with generous dollops of both professional work as a human-resources-development facilitator and community activism, which she has managed to do. "Having it all means now that no matter what the role, I'm doing it with the full focus of my being while I'm doing it, being fully present in it. It doesn't mean doing every role full time, which is an impossibility. It's not possible to stand up in front of a hundred people forty hours a week, look gorgeous, sound brilliant, and be alive when you get done. I don't want that. Neither do I want to be out organizing and mobilizing people in the community forty or fifty hours a week with no financial return to myself, because what I contribute financially to this family is important to me. It's also clear to me that I don't want to be home full time with my kids. Given my personality and my need to be involved in a lot of different things, I'm not convinced it would even be good for them, and I know it wouldn't be good for me."

Life still isn't perfect, Deanne admits, "but I think we've made tremendous progress, and I credit the hard work of women and supportive men for that. I think the definition of success really has changed, for men also, which is wonderful. My husband tells the story of going out to lunch with a number of male colleagues from different companies shortly after Douglas was born. They were in a restaurant, and they all spent the time talking about their children and their involvement with them. A woman at the next table leaned over to Ted and said, 'Please excuse me, but I've been eavesdropping, and I don't believe the conversation I'm hearing. I am delighted!' Ted said it was the best conversation he had ever had."

Although that particular incident occurred about four years ago, Ted still spends a great deal of his social/business time talking about the family, Deanne says. "He's probably my best marketing agent! For himself, he left a high-technology job that he'd been in for eleven years for a financial service-industry job. He made the shift in part because it was clear that if he stayed, there would be limited family time. It would be Workaholism 102. A decade ago, he wouldn't have taken the risk. He wouldn't have known that it was okay, and he wouldn't have known some people who have made similar choices. He would have been terrified, I think, to talk about it publicly, and I would have been, too! I think it's significantly different now. People are more willing to talk about the ways they're balancing roles, and they're more willing to talk about what doesn't work, too, and to try something new."

When she speaks at colleges, Deanne says, she finds that young women are making the assumption that they can have it all. "What I want to say to them is, 'You need to figure out what you mean by that. What does having it all mean to you specifically?' Fifteen or twenty years ago, I don't think women thought that way. They weren't encouraged to think about what their life plans looked like, where they expected to be in five years or ten years. I think women do much more of that now, and I would encourage young women to do it increasingly. Yes, I do think things are substantially different now, and I'm really proud to have been a part of it."

* * *

Eleta, while she recognizes the impossibility and undesirability of performing multiple full-time roles, is another who has chosen to have it all simultaneously. Always active and energetic, Eleta initially combined marriage with full-time work and part-time graduate school, juggling these aspects of her life adroitly for several years while she obtained a master's degree in education, taught first in the inner city and then in a rural school, then completed a Ph.D. in guidance and counseling while working part-time in a university admissions office. When a full-time position opened up in the institutions career planning and placement office, Eleta pounced on the opportunity to do counseling work, which she very much enjoyed, on a college campus, her preferred work environment. As soon as she completed her dissertation, however, she became pregnant and realized that she must find a new way to balance the pieces of her life. Though she had a full-time position at the time, she felt fairly certain she would want to work only half-time after the baby was born, so she devised a strategy to achieve that objective.

"First of all, I didn't tell anybody I was pregnant for quite a while. I had a great time surprising everybody when I told them I was four and a half months pregnant. The other thing I did to switch from full-time to part-time was to plan a careful strategy for when I told my administrators, how I was going to do it, and what I was going to propose. I felt that they would be more likely to listen to a concrete proposal than just my saying, 'Well, guess what? I'm pregnant, and I think I'll want to come back to work.' I picked the administrator I thought would be the most supportive of me to tell first, and I went in and laid out my plan for breaking my present job in half, since my goal was to work twenty hours a week. I set out what I would accomplish in twenty hours and what they would need to get somebody else to do to cover the other half of the job. I was in the fortunate position of being the supervisor of graduate students who were coming in as interns, so I was able to propose several people that I knew were there who could come in and be my 'other half.'"

After getting one administrator on her side, Eleta proceeded to meet with the two others in the office, after which the three administrators put their heads together with the university's personnel officer. "After a day of my waiting to find out what happened, they came to me and said yes, they thought they would probably be able to work that out. We cleared up all the details, and they actually found somebody to fill the other half of the position—in fact, one of the people that I had suggested—so that turned out really well."

Following the birth of her child, Eleta didn't think she would want to work full-time right away, but she remained totally committed to her career. Accommodating her new multiple roles would be difficult but worth it, she felt. "I knew I loved the work I was doing. I liked the office I was in and the people I was working with, and I knew that I would flourish by wearing a couple of hats. Let's face it, I'd been working and going to school plus being married for some time, so I knew I liked wearing several hats and that it would be very, very difficult for me to have to make a choice between working full time or being at home full time. It would be better for me if I could have some of both.

Though her self-knowledge allowed Eleta to devise a plan to accommodate conflicting needs, her definition of "having it all" still changed drastically after her first child arrived. "I had figured that I would go back to work part-time shortly after the baby was born and that within a year or so, I'd be ready to go back full-time, be a mother quite capably, and be very content. But though I was very happy at work, I found I was also very happy at home with my kid, and I had not realized how totally absorbing that was going to be for me. I just loved having her! So it became clear to me that I didn't want to go back full time. For me, to have it all was to be able to have some of everything. There is this tremendous array of choices, but we've got to recognize that at different times in our lives, different choices are appropriate, and having it all may be more of a life-span kind of thing than just a right-here-and-now thing."

While Eleta recognizes that she would not be happy with herself if she tried to work full time right now, because she wants to be with her kids, she is quick to acknowledge that it is an individual choice. "For some other women, having it all is knowing that there's a possibility of going back to work but preferring to be at home right now. For other women, having it all might mean working full time and knowing they have that child to go home to in the evenings and weekends. But for me, very definitely, having it all is having parts of everything and waiting for the children to grow a bit. Then I would expect to go back into full-time work and begin to move ahead in my field."

The advent of children, along with changes in their work lives, drew Eleta's attention to the domestic double standard, she says, although she and her husband had always shared household duties meticulously until they became parents. "For the first eleven years of our marriage, we really did try to share the chores. We split them up by month. We took turns cooking; we took turns grocery shopping; and we didn't clean that much, but when we did, we generally did it together. That was when my husband was getting his Ph.D. and I was getting my Ph.D. Then we had our first child. I was working part-time, and he was working full-time, but we were still able to juggle those kinds of things because his job allowed some flexibility in terms of when he got home and so forth. When we moved to Connecticut almost four years ago, however, and he moved into a much more traditional work environment, I found that many more of the home chores began to fall on me. Periodically, we'd sit down and negotiate a bit, and he'd pick up some chores, but then I'd find that we were slipping away from sharing again."

More recently, Eleta says, her husband experienced a work crunch, so she told him she would take on everything at home while it lasted. "I knew he needed to be able to concentrate on his work, so I just did it. But then I began to feel that we were getting more and more into that and might never get back to sharing, so we sat down a couple of weeks ago and had a long talk." With two children and two jobs to juggle these days, the pair had a lot to talk about, especially since both Eleta and her husband believe parenting means daily involvement with their children. "I don't treat my children as though they ought to just go off and play all the time while I'm home doing the chores. I want to spend time with them and do things with them, and my husband sees it that way, too. So we renegotiated all the chores, and we decided that we'd sit down on Sunday evenings and say, 'What needs to be done this week?' and 'Who will take what and do it?' That seems to be working much more effectively, and I've suddenly found that life has gotten easier! Working as much as he was, he was just having trouble staying on top of what needed to be done, and we were having trouble communicating about that. By clarifying what needs to be done each week, he isn't distant from it and unsure. It's helped tremendously, and I'd say we're back to a better balance on the home front."

Agreements like Eleta's with her husband continue to be relatively few and far between, however. For the moment, the domestic double standard lives on, complicating the lives of women who are trying to have it all either sequentially or simultaneously. A major reason that it exists is the lingering disparity in men's and women's earning power in most fields, with the result that men's time on the job is still considered more "valuable" than women's, leaving her holding the domestic fort. Another is society's continued traditional perception of each partner's role.

"I have to remind myself constantly that this isn't just my responsibility, that Al can also help do these things," says Rosemary. "The women that I know that are more assertive seem to have more of an egalitarian relationship with their husbands, but it still usually falls on the women to make sure it's all working out. I see women as being the monitors of the marriage. The men are concentrating on their jobs, but the women are organizing it so it all comes together, because we have more perspective. I think the domestic double standard will crumble as more and more women assert their rights in marriages. It's a slow, evolutionary process, but things have improved for me compared with, say, my mother, who always did everything. I probably do 70 percent of the household stuff, and Al does 30 percent, but it's an improvement.

Yes, there are improvements, and that's good. I noticed the other evening that even the notorious lady in the Enjoli television commercial was singing, "I can bring home the bacon, fry it up in the pan, but now and then, you've got to give me a hand!" It's still far from a perfect message, but there's at least some evidence of enlightenment.

Whether a woman decides to have it all at once or one step at a time is an individual decision, and the extent to which she eliminates the domestic double standard in her household is largely dependent on her individual actions. This, perhaps, is how it should be during this second stage of the women's movement.

I have never been particularly impressed with the committee system, which produces, according to Robert T. Reilly, a host of "stout beginnings, but no conclusions." Say what you will, when it comes to getting a thing done, assertive individual action beats the democratic process every time—which is not to say I would prefer to live in a dictatorship. It's just that now and then, I long for clearcut, decisive action to right the wrongs, to clear things up, to put into place *now* the institutions, policies, and legislation we know will eventually come into being in this nation of fair-minded souls, like the ERA, for instance—a prime example of the committee system at work. Stout beginnings, no conclusions.

Forgive me Phyllis, Betty, Gloria, *et al*, but somewhere along the way, I stopped believing that equal rights for women will be established any time soon in the courts, the state legislatures, or the Congress. Women do not yet have sufficient clout in these institutions, and clout is what's needed. As an individual woman, I have no power to persuade this country's political entities to my point of view, and time has proven that women *en masse* don't yet have it either. What I do have is a husband, a son, and a daughter with whom my opinion carries weight, to whom my needs and the quality of my life matter, as theirs do to me. Within this small arena, I have some clout, and I firmly believe that here I will accomplish more to further male/female equality than I could were I to join a dozen committees, march in two dozen parades. The equal rights issues will be effectively addressed where most significant interaction occurs in this country or any other—in the home, one family at a time.

I have come to see that it is absurd to believe that we can change the attitudes, ingrained since childhood, of the generations of men born before us. We may succeed in compelling them to comply with equal rights legislation at some future time, but we cannot make them like it. In our own and younger generations, though, we have a genuine opportunity to demonstrate by individual example what's in equality for men, too—the mutual freedom of role choices, the sharing of economic as well as domestic burdens, resentment-free relationships, and increased options for every family member.

I suggest, therefore, that we begin by addressing, one woman at a time, the inequities in our households that I term the "domestic double standard." Every task, every meal, every holiday, birthday, weekend errand, Cub Scout meeting, dirty diaper, checkbook register, laundry basket, and shopping list is a tool with which individual women can help those who love us, and whom we love, to discover the innumerable benefits of shared responsibility between the sexes at home.

There are more specific things each of us can do. First and foremost, we can adopt an expectation of equality, making it clear through our conversation and actions that we do not consider domestic responsibilities entirely ours, that those who share in the comforts of home are expected to share in homely tasks and are not, by doing so, helping *us*. We can vote in favor of pertinent legislation, write to our senators and Congressional representatives. We can question our employers about flexible schedules and day-care assistance and express our needs and preferences wherever they are likely to be heeded—and even where they are not. We can endorse companies, TV shows, advertisements, movies, and stores that offer products, services, and messages that erode the domestic double standard; and we can object—in person, by telephone, or in writing—to those that perpetuate it. While working to improve our options over the long term, we can ferret out and take advantage of the options we have right now. We can stop thinking of ourselves as victims and can take charge, make good choices, decide what's best for ourselves. Above all, we can laugh more, hug more—love more. A humorless, unloving shrew is unlikely to persuade anyone to her point of view or to become a desirable role model.

Once we become accustomed to doing these things, we will find ourselves effecting positive changes within and outside of our families. And as we do, every small victory will be carried forward into the next generation and the next until domestic equality is no more subject to debate than is the Golden Rule.

Eleta put it very well, I think. "We don't have to say we're stuck with what we've got right now," she pointed out. "The fact of the matter is that we can sit down and assess what we have, what we want, what our alternatives are, and then we can make choices to change." I agree.

I do not propose that we turn our homes into

battlegrounds, merely that we make full use of the opportunities that present themselves in the natural course of events to correct inequities and to prevent their perpetuation. I may have little faith in the committee system's ability to eradicate the domestic double standard, but I will never underestimate the power of *a* woman to work out a way to have it all without having to do it all.

INDEX